Ch

Jeremy Void

Other books by Jeremy Void

Derelict America
(short stories and essays)

Nefarious Endeavors
(short stories and poetry)

Smash a Lightbulb:
Poetry for Lowlifes
(poetry, prose, creative essays, and more)

Erase Your Face:
The SkullFuck Collection
(visual poetry)

Just a Kid
(experimental prose and poetry)

Sex Drugs & Violence:
Incomplete Stories for the Incomplete Human
(incomplete stories)

An Art Form:
The Crass Poetry Collection
(poetry)

My Story:
The Short Version
(my own drunkalogue)

I Need Help:
The SkullFuck Collection
(visual poetry)

The Lost Letters
(poetry)

Chaos

Writing

Jeremy Void

Chaos Writing

ISBN Number:

978-0-578-17385-6

ChaosWriting **Press**

IT'S A MINDFUCK

www.chaoswriting.net

To Vanessa Lauren

IMPORTANT MESSAGE

PLEASE READ

- ❖ I am not a writer nor an artist, I'm just a mere fabricator of bullshit. I represent no cause.

- ❖ Throughout this book I frequently mention my attendance at AA (Alcoholics Anonymous). But be rest assured, I do not represent the rooms in any way, nor do I represent anything, for that matter. My singularity is terminal and I belong nowhere.

- ❖ If I happen to have mentioned you specifically, with an angry pretense, keep in mind that I hate no one, the hateful words expressed here are only products of my momentary rage that had passed as soon as I put it down on paper. You see, I use writing to heal my wounds, and it works very well. So please try not to get upset with me if you see your name in this book, and if you happen to anyway, try writing about it!—it really does good for the soul. Trust me, I know.

Enjoy!!!

Contents

Say NO to saying YES

Say YES to saying NO

Selected Rants & Ramblings:

Introduction

My writing started out very standardized—that was back when I was learning how to write. I taught myself grammar solely from reading and writing and experimenting with punctuation. It just came naturally to me. My dad had said, "For someone who did so poorly in high school, how are you so good with grammar?"

It just came naturally to me.

That was back when I was learning how to write, you see.

But now I've learned how to write and I've figured out the English language. Some people say that takes a whole lifetime to do, but for me, it only took a few years because I have a very simple rule of thumb when it comes to grammar:

What are my objectives?

If I want my writing to confuse the reader, for example, I must use punctuation to accomplish such a fete. I must mold the words and the punctuation to fit my objectives.

Jeremy Void

Using words and punctuation intentionally as opposed to accidentally.

So now I'm a writer. But knowing how to write and use words masterly like I have wasn't enough to satisfy the young writer I have become. It just wasn't enough.
So I threw the rules out the window.
I took a hammer to standardizations.
I broke the English language, turned it on its side, and kicked it as hard as I could. I took a knife to its face and scribbled all over its skin. And in doing so I realized there is so much more for me to learn. I had to unlearn what I had taught myself, I had to unlearn format and style and everything that made up the English language.

As long as my rule of thumb still applied: **What are my objectives?**

If I met my objectives then I'm a success, the way I see it.

But you must know the rules before you can break them!
 but you must know the rules before you can break them!
  but you must know the rules before you can break them!
    SUCCESFULLY

In order for me to unlearn writing, I had to learn it. In order for me to deconstruct the English language, I had to construct it in the first place.

SO there you go. I hope you enjoy this book....

introduction2

Dear Reader,

you see, i have Borderline Personality Disorder which is very similar to Bipolar, in that i suffer from two different poles:

> there is **Mania**
> there is <u>Depression</u>
> > & rarely do I ever tread
> between the two

but the major difference is: Borderline Personality Disorder is dependent entirely on environmental circumstances, as in
if things in my life are going swimmingly
> **then you bet my emotional state will be thru the roof; i will be Manic, altho what with the medications i take, my Mania is usually more in the range of hypo-Mania,**
> **which is a lesser Mania:**
> > ❖ **i might talk alot**
> > ❖ **my mind might race supersonic**
> > ❖ **my eyes might be pried wide open**

Jeremy Void

**but rarely do i go beyond that
i mean, im not exactly stealing ambulances or anything in
this state..........................**

then theres the other side of the coin:
<u>when things in my life seem
lower than normal i have a
tendency to sink, mood-wise
i get quite Depressed</u>

<u>like anyone else on the face of this planet i am known to
get down on myself from time to time, only
i get exponentially down
lower than the average human
being</u>

<u>which entails lots & lots of relentless brooding that can
get tiresome & lonely & maybe even boring at times.......</u>

this is how Borderline Personality Disorder got its name:
its Borderline Psychotic   i act Psychotic, what with
the frequent shifting of emotions

remember, my
mood is entirely
depended on envi-
ronmental
circumstances

**   ⧖   **

XVI

Chaos Writing

SO   that said, things in this book may very well drop into the <u>Southern Hemisphere,</u> and they may very well rise into the **Northern Hemisphere**, but that isn't to say I don't have days that do in fact tread between the North and South Poles; it's just rare, is all.

So, some of what is contained in this book is <u>dark</u> and <u>depressing,</u> and some of it is **bright** and **uplifting.**

In reading this, try not to take one piece and assume that it speaks for me entirely.   I have many sides, which you are soon to find out....

SO there you go. I hope you enjoy this book....

Introduction the Third
The Poetic Version

I'm not trying to boast
gloat
or complain
....Don't read this thinking
      I wonder what Jeremy Void
         is like in real life
      I wonder how Jeremy Void
         thinks about things on his own time
cuz no one cares about that anyway
and if you do if you are in fact curious
about who I am as a person
and about the things that I do in my life
well, guess what
      this is the right book for you.

But for the others
for the selfish herd
the ones who can't think of anyone
but themselves, which is
      I'm afraid
the mass majority of us
      you should treat this book like
      a mirror, like a portal

Jeremy Void

like a telescope pointed inward......
In reading this you should try to think
of the ways in which you can relate to me
cuz I know there are more of us out there
cuz I know I'm not alone you're not alone
we're all so similar it's scary, isn't it????

The specific instances mentioned here
don't mean shit without
a body that comes with a mind,
although some bodies don't some people are
just plain mindless don't you know
        about that?

I give you my soul I give you my heart
I give you a mind that doesn't seem to quit
a body connected to legs connected to
feet that don't stop thumping the floor
        beneath me.

I give you a story about
a man a boy a kid and a clueless adult
mixed up and confused and lost and hungry
a soul so full of scorn it's like I'll die
angry and filled with remorse
and I'm afraid that that fate might be so true
it pisses me off even more so I'm afraid....

THIS BOOK represents
more than words
more than pictures
more than just a few cheesy lines
it represents me and my entirety

XX

Chaos Writing

my journey my blossoming
my evolution through darkness and into
the light >>>>>>>>>>>>>>>>>>>>>>>>>>>>>>>>

It shows me at low points
it shows me at high points
it shows me here there
and everywhere
and it shows you just one step behind
just one step ahead
or maybe even directly beside me
as I walk down a path layered with scorn
and it shows me lost
and it shows me finding my way through
a world filled with let-downs
set-backs
people who have kicked me around
people who have lifted me up
and people who simply have
turned the other cheek
at the sight of me
because they simply want
nothing to do with me

But FUCK EM
because this is me
this is you
and as I lead you on my journey
through a twisted world
I promise you you won't come out
the same
and neither will I....

SO I HOPE
—I really do—
I hope
you enjoy this book.

it begins

I've been accused of only writing for the sake of being successful by a few different people in my life, but let the record be straight

I LOVE TO WRITE

but I'm not gonna lie, there is a big part of me that wants to make it as a famous writer, to get ahead, to become a household name, even

WHY?

I've got nothing else going for me

I've had shit luck all my life, finding that I just suck at everything I've ever done

and on top of that my peers rejected me, and continue to reject me even today—because I'm just awkward in social situations, I guess—and I have no prospects for girls at the present moment, surrounded by happy-go-lucky married couples that, frankly, make me sick-to-boot

so if I don't make it at this

I will die a fucking failure....
Is that what you want?

Another Sleepless Rant

Two nights without sleep is never good for the soul. For the body. But right now, at the present moment, I feel as refreshed as a fresh turd. I read some poetry which triggered the muse within and here I am, spewing vile onto the page again. But lovely vile it is. I guess you could say I'm bored, I'm always bored; I guess you could say I'm angry, *Pfff,* I'm always fucking angry, guess you could say. This guy pissed me off, I don't like your face, your stomach reminds me of a punching bag and I just want to slug it, blat blat blat.

The hour is 1:30 AM and when I say this is the second night in a row without sleep, I kid you not. I'm scared shitless for tomorrow because tomorrow I gotta see the dentist and find out what happened to my disintegrated tooth. It melted disintegrated or fell out, one way or another it's not there and something's wrong. I baled on the cleaning because I was afraid of what they might tell me, what they might find, how they might scoff and scowl in an oh so scrutinizing manner and I would feel like a dipshit thinking what the hell is wrong with me. So I baled and my teeth decayed some more and now tomorrow I gotta face the music and find out what happened to my tooth.

I gotta piss really badly but I'm holding it in till this rant
is finished. I don't see the point, just another book by
Jeremy Void to not sale and get zero royalties. I made $5
tonight in donations off the samplers, so I guess that's
something.

Went to the open-mike in a cheery mood ready to read
some new poetry when I ran into friends and Baby
Taker was going to play they told me and this was cool I
thought, but when they played I felt a tremendous bomb
erupt in my gut and I had to leave. It was BJ man. Fucking BJ. Thinks he's so cool the way he shouts and scowls
saying wanna hear us *not* play music? I spat on him
while he was thrashing before the stage not once maybe
twice but most likely three times and nobody noticed
and that made me even more mad. I wanted somebody
to see me do it so I'd look badass in my original T-shirt
that said BLEED FOR ME. But nobody saw and this only
served to piss me off even more.

But do you know what made me the most mad of all? He
was like me, just like me, cocky and arrogant and so full
of semen it was like he had a dick for a head just spurt-
ing semen and it rained down on us like a water fountain, big mountainous spurts gushing up and then coming down and we danced in the raining cum. Gross,
right? He had a face that I wanted to cold cock, a stomach that I wanted to uppercut, and an attitude that I
wanted to cut down and reveal him for the snake that he
was.
He's a chameleon, that part's obvious——fake and willing
to do just about anything to show that he's real//
like me

Another Sleepless Rant

So I left and I was angry and I went home and I was angry and I went on my computer, read some d. a. levy,
worked on my books, and then magically the anger subsided and now I feel relieved, only I really gotta piss, so
that's enough out of me—   for now.

The Slanted Truth

In a world filled to the brink with filthy politicians I've gotta stand tall, stand above, do my best to not get lost in their rhetoric, their rhetorical rubbish—I wipe my ass with it. I live alone in my apartment where I'm immersed in books and fruit flies (but those are another story)—and I don't watch the news, read the newspaper, get lost in the tabloids, I just don't fucking care who's fucking who—politics is really just an orgy, don't you know? He fucked she, she fucked he, they all fucked each other in their oh so homoerotic white house—I'd love to spray-paint a swastika on that, a hammer-and-sickle to support the commie turds (Che Guevara would be very proud to see that his hard work had paid off and somebody still cares about his cause, but fuck Che Guevara, he was a preacher, a pseudo-revolutionary, who had achieved nothing—and besides, I happen to like Capitalism). Fuck them all and drown them in their own wasted existences. Hang them up and beat em with an inch of their lives—just to hear the truth, that's all I want from them.

But in a world where everything is fabricated by Facebook, is truth a real entity, or a demon of the past? Did truth ever exist to begin with? You got '80s punks screaming about how they want the truth. You got '70s punks screaming that they've had enough of the lie. In the '60s there were hippies without clothing wandering around high on acid saying they want the truth. (What truth? You're an acid head, you wouldn't know the truth if it pissed on your hairy face.)

So what's the point if there are no truths? Well, except for those of Facebook and Wikipedia, because any idiot with a computer can speak their opinion on just about any subject. (Thank you very much, Social Media. As a result of your totally selfless kindness I'm getting reamed out by guys who couldn't even write themselves out of a paper bag, who think they have the merits to hassle me about my own writing.)

Just remember kids
when push comes to shove
when the shit hits the fan
when the crowd scrambles and runs
for cover, just remember this:

There are no truths anymore
There are no lies
Everything's equivalent
No one's right
Everyone's wrong
It's a fact

Feel free to check my sources on that. They're legit.

WORKS CITED:

Facebook
Wikipedia
Deviant Art

A Stark Realization

I realized something last night. I don't know if it's good that I realized this, or if it will just play out as another tumultuous roll in my useless life.

Maybe a year ago, or more, I wrote a short story called "Bloody Harry," which is the second-to-last story in *Nefarious Endeavors.*.
What's interesting about this story is the state of mind I was in when I wrote it.
You see,

- I can't write when I'm drunk, let alone have a single deep thought,
- and I always thought that stimulants didn't help my creative process either, because, speedy, I take on too many tasks at once, and thus can't dedicate the majority of my time to focusing on my writing.

That's what I thought,
but after "Bloody Harry" I realized that's not a very true statement, saying I can't write while spun,
because that's the state I was in when I wrote the story.

Let me break it down for you:

"Bloody Harry" starts with the protagonist, Harry himself, departing from his job. He's a banker, and he's quite
happy, and everyone in town seems to love him.
Then Harry meets a girl, a Punk rocker named Sherry,
who has a boyfriend and calls herself straight edge.
Which doesn't exactly fly for Harry, an oversexed man
who seldom gets turned down by women.

Now   fast-forward a bit >>
The two of them become friendly with one another, or
more than friendly, the way Harry sees it.

Then   fast-forward some more >>
Harry loses it.. Goes crazy. Ape shit.

You see,
this is one of my longer stories. And Harry isn't me, in
fact. He's so different from me that it would seem almost impossible that I'd created him so vividly like I did.
I can't be *that* good.
                              Well, news flash: I am.
                              Period
But when I depicted this character, typing those first
couple sentences on my laptop—
                    "Harry punched
                    his employee ID in
                    the touchscreen
                    computer, clocking
                    out of work. As he
                    left the bank he
                    said goodbye to all
                    his coworkers."
—I was spun.

A Stark Realization

SPUN

I was happy happy happy / Harry was happy happy happy/// As the drug took its magnificent but brain-crushing course, I banged the keyboard hard and fast, words strung up on my screen faster than my heart could beat—

and at the time, that was *fast.*

Then, the initial glee was sweated out of me, my high wearing down at an alarming rate, myself suddenly cued in to every last inch of my body, my brain left with one final stitch of sanity that stretched and stretched and stretched, as time progressed.

(I wrote that story—all 6,276 words of it—in a good forty-five minutes. Can you believe it?)

But here's the catch:

That I was spun
means nothing to
me—*Nada.* Well, not
anymore, at least.

I'm starting to think that sleep deprivation was the real cause.

Look, I got no sleep last night, and I wrote all this in less than the length of a full AA meeting. I hadn't journaled a long entry like this one in ages; and wait until you see what I came up with in the middle of the night and this morning, the shit I pulled out of my imagination, which is probably inflating like a bubble right now, growing larger, which puts it under extreme pressure, and one of these days it will snap—I'm sure of it....

But until then, I should use my ultra-traumatized mind as much as humanly possible///

Just Be Yourself

Tomorrow I am going to serenade a random girl with a poem I wrote tonight. I have no girl in mind though; I'm just curious if all this hype about being yourself actually works in a real life situation. If it's not limited to the kinds of things therapists say when you get rejected, when people piss and shit all over you and you come into the session crying and feeling terrible, and your therapist, a decent-looking man, funny, fun-loving, and smart, looks you square in the eye and says,

"Just be yourself."

Well, Mr. Therapist, if it was that simple, I'd have one million dollars and girls hanging all over me. If all that hype in movies about happy endings and all that crud was actually true, wowee. I'd be rich, in love, and happy for once. But the problem is, in real life there are no happy endings, everything continues forward, going on and on and on,,,,,,,, and the only way out, the only ending I'm aware of, is a black hearse or a black yearn. One or the other, you will die, you will suffer, and you will rot. The only ending is death. DEATH.

A bed in a coffin or a terroriz-
ing blaze of fire——yum yum
yum yum yum!

But that isn't to say life is all bad, cuz it's not—I've just had a bad week, and I will get to that. Tonight I sulked, I counseled a friend of mine who was going through a rough time too via Facebook, I sulked some more, and then I met a nice woman who was a little bitter about me posting something not about Patti Smith in a Patti Smith fan club/group. I posted it—with which I plan to serenade a random girl tomorrow—because after I wrote it, I read a poem by Patti Smith, thought it sounded similar to the one I just wrote, and thus figured Patti Smith fans would enjoy it.

Well, I guess not: rejected and denied for being myself once again....

But at least she wasn't a dick about it, and we spoke a bit—and that's when all my spirits flipped (and I know they'll plunge again sometime soon——☹)   :::: She once knew Richard Hell; *knew* being the key word there. Knew, being the closest I've ever come to speaking to him, to my idol—*my fucking idol*—and all of you know I've searched endlessly and relentlessly for his contact info just so I could shoot him a hello and an ego boost that he inadvertently saved my life—not that he needs an ego boost or anything.

And now you know—the cat is out of the basket. Not that it was a secret or anything....

Now let me backtrack. How'd the week start? Who'd piss me off this time? Was it my neighbor? My friend? My lover, my wife on the side (haha)? Oh yeah, that's who. It was me. I did it—no surprise there—I am my own worst enemy, always throwing the wrench into my own fucked-up life. The following is so true it fucking scares me to death:

> *every girl i meet wants to fuck me, every guy i*
> *meet wants to fight me. i say things i regret but*
> *constantly tell myself i meant it. stand strong &*
> *proud & turn the other cheek on your fellow man*
> *is my motto, & yet im so quick to help out the vic-*
> *tim of persecution which i guess makes me a*
> *hypocrite, but a good hypocrite, a hypocrite who*
> *pushes negative vibes but acts nicely & kindly to*
> *everyone. i hate the nice me & wish to be the*
> *mean me but the truth of the matter is i cudnt*
> *hurt a fly———unless it bites me & then i will be*
> *the first to smash it dead. im a typical borderline*
> *case: i hate everybody but im always lonely &*
> *desperate for attention. im the first to tell you*
> *how much i love you, but deep down inside i hate*
> *you & want you dead, only if you died id miss you*
> *terribly, cuz whats the saying? Distance makes*
> *the heart grow stronger & fonder & i end up beat-*
> *ing myself up (& off) until youre here & when i*
> *get you i toss you out the window hoping you land*
> *on your head. ask Kristen, who im sure you know,*
> *all about it & shell tell you shes been the victim of*
> *my insanity time & time again, but she loves me*
> *anyway & i keep pulling her my way—except for*
> *one time, when she did the pulling for a change—&*
> *because shes so quick to forgive me all the time i*
> *feel as if shes my perfect girlfriend & i want to*
> *marry her, unless i kill her first, in which case i*
> *will cry & cry until i meet somebody else & then*
> *forget all about her. a week passes & everybodys*
> *gone & im alone & beating myself black-&-blue at*

*how stupid i was for destroying such a good thing.
but soon after, i find something else i can stick my
dick into, stir it around like its a pot of stew, pull
out, & shoot. thats my life.*
                Welcome to Hell!

Yeah I know. It can't be that bad. Well it is. Get used to
it, because this is who I am this is my sickness and if you
don't like it, stop reading this!—not that anyone is actually reading this crap anyway.

                    My other problem:
                    everybody hates me/

Did I say I'm my problem? No, everybody's my problem;
they just don't know it yet and don't exactly care and if I
can't put the blame on anyone who will listen, I might as
well point the finger at me cuz I do care and I will listen.

            The second thing that went wrong—
God, this is the worst. I agreed to let a gorgeous model
take shots of me naked—what the hell is wrong with
me????—even though I know no one will wanna see that
anyway, and I only really did it as a much-needed ego
boost which completely backfired and now my ego is as
tiny as the dick she took pictures of. It really isn't that
small. It just appeared very small seen through my
nervous and frightened eyes that were focusing on what
they wanted to see and not what I wanted to see and
what I wanted to see was a dick that touched the floor.
That's what I see when I'm alone, anyway———
but not when this hot model and her *boyfriend,* no less,
stood before me and there was one other present—
Gawd!—and the camera was snapping and I was sweating

and cringing and cursing myself for initiating this plan in the first place—

Yes, it was my fucking fucking fucking idea—

fuck!!!

So that happened. Then that night I went and pissed a lot of people off. Partook in an argument with an extreme liberal cunt who calls herself an anarchist—*right!*—but believes picking sides is the answer. I believe picking sides is A answer but not THE answer, and that's the part she had a problem with—that I'm so indifferent to everything, so apathetic.

No, I am neither of the two, I am very helpful and very selfless and would run across the world for somebody I didn't exactly care for as a person—that's the kind of person I am——

although she didn't exactly see it that way cuz to her having no opinion is the worst stance to have. But why???? Is it really helpful to force your ideas down someone's throat? Or would it be a better use of my time if I held out my hand and asked them what was the matter. I don't know and I don't care. I do my part everyfuckingday—I even held out my hand for her when she messaged me via Facebook in the middle of the night saying she was going to kill herself....

But, as she soon figured out, *Words are my weapon, and if you piss me off, I will murder you. I COULD break it to you nicely, and I would, but if you piss me off, then I won't.*

PLAIN AND SIMPLE

But it's not like I do that intentionally or anything; I just
get mad and attack. I fly off the handle and stab you repeatedly. Stab stab stab until you're dead—like that. And
then I stab you some more. I can't help it, I just black
out. It happens, but I'm not sorry for it, ever, unless
your name is Kristen
in which case I am very very sorry for everything I've
ever done to you and I'm sorry for all the torment I am
going to put you through in the future—assuming we'll
speak again—and what I'm sorry for the most is that
when you come into the picture I lose my desire to be
good and it becomes all about me. I can't help it. You do
that to me and my dick reflexes kick in. My head is
irrelevant then. That's what I hate the most about myself—that I can't even be good and genuine to the one
girl that matters most.
They say you hurt the ones you love the most; well on
account that I seem to hurt everyone so damn much so
damn often
Kristen is shit out of luck.
                              I'm so sorry for this ail-
ment that haunts me day in day out.
Just think
            when I say to you something downright mean,
            sexually driven, and that hits like a
            sledgehammer across your face, I'm the one
            who suffers, not you. I have to live with my-
            self, not you. I wish you did but I'd just drive
            you away so damn quick....

Fucked by the Law
A Brief Lesson in History

I don't remember what year Lethal Erection formed, nor do I even remember how old I was. I was either 17 or 18 when we formed, and I was either 17 or 18 when we played our first show at the Hyde Center, in Newton Highlands, MA. We headlined the show because the point of the show was to raise money to keep me out of jail. We made a little over $200, and I needed $700 in all. It was as close as I could get. But our original bassist, who we called Harry Erection, stole all the proceeds, the slimy bastard. The original lineup was me, Jeremy St. Chaos, on vocals; Jeremy Acid on guitar; Harry Erection on bass; and Johnny Pain (or JP, for short) on drums. Harry left the band first, for the aforementioned reasons. And because, he said later on, he thought we were a joke and didn't want to play for us anymore.

At the time, I was going out with a girl who I thought of as a goddess, whose name was Kristen, and we eventually called her Kristen Epileptic because after one show, before which we blew a ton of cocaine, she complained again and again that she couldn't play well because her hands were shaking too badly; so I deemed her Kristen Epileptic.

I think I was going out with her when the band started—or soon after we started, at least.

She dabbled with the bass, and since she was my girlfriend I taught her a bunch of Lethal Erection songs. At one show, after which people said it reminded them of *Media Blitz* by the Germs, I drank a shit-ton of whiskey while my band set up. By the time the show was about to start, and we were about to go on, for we were on first, I wrapped one arm around a good friend of mine, Johnny, who took my part in helping the band set up, and another arm around Kristen and led the two of them up to the door and slurred something along the lines of, These are the two loves of my life, they're getting in for free. Then I released Johnny from my embrace and dragged Kristen closer to the stage and yelled, Somebody get her a bass, and somebody did, and we were good to go, although for the most part her amp stayed on silent, just like Sid.

At the end of the show, every member of Lethal Erection was bleeding: Instead of a bass pick Kristen used a nickel and cut herself on the strings; Jeremy Acid played bass guitar for another band, the singer of which attacked him during their set, and the neck of his guitar split open the side of his face; and apparently I whacked JP in the mouth with the microphone, which I don't remember doing, for I blacked out during our entire set.

How I was bleeding? No one seems to know. We filmed the whole thing, and the moron in charge of filming steadied the camera on the stage the whole time, as opposed to following the singer as he stalked around in the crowd like most Punk DVDs do. The closest theory we could come up with was: I got into a fight with the mike stand and lost, I was so drunk. JP said he looked up from the drum set and saw me strangling the mike stand, looked back down at his drums, and then looked up again, and there I was, lying prone on the ground with the mike stand on top of me and a thin line of blood dribbling down my bottom lip.

JP left the band shortly after that, for a girl, I think, though I'm not too sure. I think his girlfriend didn't approve of him playing in a Punk rock band. Jeremy left the band because he had two jobs and was presently in another band as well, and he just simply didn't have time for Lethal Erection.

So that left just me and Kristen, and the band sort of went on hiatus, during which time people had repeatedly told me to keep at it because I was Lethal Erection, *me*. I should get a whole new lineup, they would say. I searched for new members everywhere. I found a few people who said they were interested, but not interested enough, I would soon find out.

Then I met Chuck, who we eventually called De-Chuck-Tive, because next to me, he was the most DESTRUCTIVE person I've ever met. I met him when I attended New England Institute of Art for Audio Production, although he claimed to have met me when the Business played at Club Lido maybe a year earlier. I guess I just wasn't entirely present at that show, because I didn't remember him. Chuck was wearing a flannel shirt with

a large Generation X back patch sewn on. I approached
him first, and he said he met me before, though I
couldn't remember. He told me he played guitar and
said he'd be interested in joining Lethal Erection.

Also, Kristen knew this guy, more of a fat loser
than anything, named Pat, who said he'd drum for us.
The first practice with the new lineup took place at Pat's
house in Southern New Hampshire. Since Chuck lived in
Haverhill, MA, which is right on the border of Massachusetts and New Hampshire, I took the train to the Haverhill stop and he drove us the rest of the way there. This
is how our friendship began: I got off the train and de-
scended the stairs into the parking lot. Shortly after entering the lot, a red pickup truck came barreling at me
and would have hit me too, if I hadn't jumped out of the
way. Then it stopped beside me and I saw that it was
Chuck. As we left the parking lot together, I asked him,
Mind if I drink? and he said, No, not at all, and then
pulled a bottle of Jäger out of the backseat. I had a bottle of Jim Beam and he had a bottle of Jäger—each's own
favorite drink.

Also, I had a bag of coke for when Kristen got
there, because I owed her, I guess. And since Chuck
hadn't done any before, I hooked him up with a free line,
and boy, did he love it. Pat, who I found out later had
never done the stuff either, told me he had in fact done
it before, and therefore got none.

So it was me, Chuck, and Kristen—we were Lethal
Erection. I was no longer the only member. What made
us the band was our reckless, fuck-off attitudes that no

one seemed to match. No member after that could put up with us. Most of them tried, and all of them failed.

What happened to Pat was we kicked him out for being a douchebag. He hated me because I was with Kristen, I guess, and he had a total crush on her.

So, now you know. That's how Lethal Erection came about.

Interview—Lethal Erection
as seen on YouTube

Interviewer: **Fink**
Interviewees: **De-Chuck-Tive**
and **Jeremy St. Chaos** (me)

They're all drunk, in **Fink's** old kitchen, **Jeremy St. Chaos** and **De-Chuck-Tive** sitting across from one another at the kitchen table and **Fink** hidden behind the camera. **De-Chuck-Tive** wears a black wifebeater and a pair of pleated pants, with the sleeves of his flannel wrapped and tied snugly around his waist, and his usual hat. **Jeremy St. Chaos** wears a white T-shirt that says DESTROY at the top, and has a swastika in the center, on top of an outline of an upside-down crucifix, and a pair of pinstriped black stretch jeans, also with the sleeves of his flannel wrapped and tied snugly around his waist; he wears white-rimmed sun-glasses, and his jet-black hair is charged up. **De-Chuck-Tive** drinks Jäger out of a Dunkin' Donuts Styrofoam coffee cup, and **Jeremy St. Chaos** drinks a Sparc right out of the can.

————

Fink:
Hi, we're here with the band Lethal Erection—two members.

Jeremy St. Chaos: {shouting and laughing}
The only fuckin' members!

Fink:
Alright. So let's get a … uh … let's tell us about your band.

De-Chuck-Tive:
Our band's awesome, that's about it.

Jeremy St. Chaos:
Haha—what about our band?

De-Chuck-Tive:
That's just about it, we're awesome. We like to drink, fuck shit up—

Jeremy St. Chaos: {shouting}
—fight, and fuck!

De-Chuck-Tive:
And fuck `Yeah, man. Do drugs too.

Jeremy St. Chaos:
But we ain't no GG Allin wannabes. Fuck that bullshit.

Fucked by the Law

De-Chuck-Tive:
Cuz we're Lethal Erection—

Jeremy St. Chaos: {shouting}
—and you suck! .

{**De-Chuck-Tive** laughs}

Fink:
So, when'd you get started?

De-Chuck-Tive:
Back in 1957—

Jeremy St. Chaos:
No no. No no. It was back ... um ... it was back ... um ... it was a few months before I turned 18—

De-Chuck-Tive:
Before Elvis was even born—

Jeremy St. Chaos:
Shut the fuck up!

{**De-Chuck-Tive** laughs}

Jeremy St. Chaos:
We started ... it was a few months before I turned 18, the members were me ... it started with me and Acid Jeremy—we call him Acid Jeremy cuz he looks like the fuckin' acid dealer from *SLC Punk.* His real name is Jeremy Brown ... he looked like the acid dealer. He's uh, he's uh ... the guitarist. He used to be the gui—the bassist of

Negative Insight. And he quit Negative— Well, he joined
our band because he's like, this isn't what Punk rock's all
about, Punk rock's about fucking shit up and being
snotty and disgusting and rude and shit. So he jo—me
and him started the band. My friend ... my best friend
at the time, fuckin' Harold, we eventually called him
Harry Erection. He fuckin', uh ... we said, Hey, start
fuckin' playing the bass, he played for a month, and
we're like, alright you're in the band now. Then so it was
just me, him, and ... uh, Harold at the time, me and Jeremy started that shit, Jeremy and Jeremy. And then we
found JP along the way, and I'd known this kid since he
was, like, 12, so and, uh ... I didn't even know he played
drums, and he fuckin' ... he played drums he started
playing drums for us. That's how we started. But then
shit got fucked up because I'm a fucked-up person and
people quit the band because of me. Cuz they're fuckin'
cunts, they don't know shit what they're doing.

Fink:
*Alright, so where's the places you've played around Boston? with
what bands?*

Jeremy St. Chaos:
In Boston? Or anywhere?

Fink:
Well, anywhere would go.

Jeremy St. Chaos:
We played in Newton a bunch of times, that's where I'm
from. We played once in Haverhill.

Fucked by the Law

De-Chuck-Tive:
That was the best show.

Jeremy St. Chaos:
Yeah, that was, that was one of the best shows we played.
We played down in this warehouse many times, this
abandoned, uh ... this abandoned warehouse in Everett—

De-Chuck-Tive:
The best show was when there was just three people.

Jeremy St. Chaos:
The one down ... the one down in fuckin', uh ... the one
down in Haverhill was definitely the best show. The one
down in Haverhill, okay, was the best show. We played in
that dude's apartment, that abandoned place next to,
uh—

De-Chuck-Tive:
The abandoned house party, we were the only ones playing. All the kids went fuckin' wild for us.

Jeremy St. Chaos:
And they were all fuckin' emo fags.

De-Chuck-Tive:
No, they're hardcore kids.

Jeremy St. Chaos:
No, they weren't they weren't like hardcore kids, they
were fuckin' screamo fags.

De-Chuck-Tive:
No no no no no ... no no no. The girls were, but the guys were, like, hardcore.

Jeremy St. Chaos:
No, no—

De-Chuck-Tive:
They liked bands like fuckin' Hatebreed and shit—

Jeremy St. Chaos:
They looked like fuckin'—

Fink:
Alright, enough with your story about your argument and let's get back to the interview—

Jeremy St. Chaos:
They looked like fuckin' emos who listened to hardcore.

Fink:
So, so, tell us some, uh—something about, uh ... the music you write, the lyrics, uh, what they mean to the, uh, like to the Punk scene, to the Punks.

Jeremy St. Chaos:
The lyrics mean fuck Punk rock. Fuck you, fuck you ... I'm cool, fuck you all, that's what the lyrics mean. Lethal Erection—you wanna hear the lyrics?

Fink:
Yeah, tell us some of your lyrics.

Fucked by the Law

Jeremy St. Chaos:
"All drugged up out in the heat, / ready for a fight, ready for defeat. / Out on the street with an erect mind, / a lethal voice, and a fuck you sign. / I got no time to think things through, / cuz the life I live are the choices I choose. // I'm a fucked-up kid, in a fucked-up world. / An erection hard enough to kill a girl. / Lethal.... / I'm a fucked-up man, in a fucked-up town. / The people I see are going down / ....Erection. // I don't care if you look at me / cuz it don't matter what you see. / All that matters is I'm a fuckin' screw / and later tonight I'll be fucking you. // I'm a fucked-up kid, in a fucked-up world. / An erection hard enough to kill a girl. / Lethal.... / I'm a fucked up man, in a fucked-up town. / The girls I see are going down. / ...Erection. / Lethal Erection."

Fink:
So tell me some of your influences and what made you get into the music you play.

Jeremy St. Chaos:
I don't know ... The Germs. Obviously, man.

De-Chuck-Tive:
Elvis Presley.

Jeremy St. Chaos:
The Germs for me, man.

De-Chuck-Tive:
Johnny ... Johnny Thunders and the Heartbreakers.

Jeremy St. Chaos:
The Dead Boys. Richard Hell, man—

De-Chuck-Tive:
Definitely the Dead Boys on coke. If you do coke, listen to the Dead Boys.

Jeremy St. Chaos:
Richard Hell, man. Richard Hell ... awe ... he's the only dude I'd ever fuck. He'd be the only dude I'd ... ever let go up my ass. I mean, maybe I'd fuck a dude, as long as I'm giving it to them. I ain't taking no dude up my ass.

De-Chuck-Tive:
That's like fucking a dude and saying I ain't no homo.

Jeremy St. Chaos:
Fuck it, I'd have sex with a dude ... as long as I'm giving it to him up the ass—

De-Chuck-Tive:
You're still a homo.

{**Fink** laughs}

Jeremy St. Chaos:
I don't give a fuck what it is. Richard Hell, though, I'd actually let give to me.

{**De-Chuck-Tive** laughs}

Jeremy St. Chaos:

He's the only dude I'd let do that. GG Allin though ... you know, maybe GG Allin cuz he's so small and I wouldn't feel nothing. I'd let GG Allin put it up my ass only cuz I wouldn't feel nothing. I'd just be afraid of catching his diseases and shit. I'm tested. I'm tested. Girls out there, I'm tested, I'm clean. You know, I'm clean. I've had a lot of nasty, dirty, rotten sex, but I'm fuckin' clean, so ... fuck me later. Fuck me!

Fink:

So, what—where's the band going in the future? what's your plans? what are you gonna do?

Jeremy St. Chaos:

I don't know, last time we had a band practice with our drummer, I sliced the drummer's neck open—no no no, not his neck, uh ... his sister's ... I sliced his sister's neck open, and she was bleeding, and ever since then we haven't been able to practice with our drummer cuz we got kicked out of the fuckin' house, and we haven't been able to practice, so ... we're kinda having some difficulties there, but it's just metopause.

{**De-Chuck-Tive** chuckles}

Jeremy St. Chaos:

Lethal Erection has gone flaccid. But we will become erect again. It happened once before. We went flaccid—

De-Chuck-Tive:

We're getting pretty popular on MySpace.

Jeremy St. Chaos:
Yeah, we're being pretty fuckin' popular on MySpace.
What's that shit about? Everybody fuckin' loves us. Why
aren't we playing no more shows anymore?—

De-Chuck-Tive:
Cuz we ain't trying so hard.

Jeremy St. Chaos:
But the fuck— Yeah, that's true. But this fuckin' ... our
drummer Walker, man! We need a drummer who can
stick with this shit and his sister ain't a cunt—

De-Chuck-Tive:
Who hangs out with us—

Jeremy St. Chaos:
And his sister ain't a ... he gotta have a sister who ain't a
cunt—

De-Chuck-Tive:
—and who hangs out with us.

Jeremy St. Chaos:
If we get a new drummer whose sister's a cunt, I may
accidentally slash her ... neck open again.

De-Chuck-Tive:
Unless she's hot.

Jeremy St. Chaos:
Then I may accidentally rape her.

Fucked by the Law

De-Chuck-Tive:
Exactly, that's all I'm about. What other questions do you got?

Jeremy St. Chaos:
Rape is just accidental sex—

Fink:
So what are you boys up to tonight, huh?

Jeremy St. Chaos and **Chuck:**
What?

Fink:
What are you boys up to tonight?

De-Chuck-Tive:
Drinking.

Jeremy St. Chaos: {screaming and rising to his feet and attacking the camera}
VIOLENCE!!!

{**De-Chuck-Tive** laughs}

De-Chuck-Tive: {laughing}
Keepin' him outta jail.

Jeremy St. Chaos:
Keepin' me outta jail?—I got court on Monday.

An Existential Funk

I've been in an existential funk that probably started a few months ago, but has evolved since then. I've been thinking a lot about people, or more specifically, me in regards to people. There are so many of us on this earth, all with our own agendas, stories, interests, personalities, etc. And yet—I am me, stuck as me, forever doomed to this shell of a body that is mine. It's not that I'm unhappy with myself—or maybe I am a little— but that being stuck in a single body is just so inhibiting. I want to know more, to be more; I don't want to be human anymore. I want to experience life through another set of eyes; I want to remember a past that isn't mine.

This thought, which, as I said above, came to me months ago, has been haunting me, in that I have tried to will my soul, if such a thing even exists, up and out of my shell and into someone else's. Yet every attempt has failed. No surprise there. The only thing that keeps me somewhat sane is that everyone else is stuck in their own body too, and if I wasn't me, but someone else, I would be in the same predicament.

Why me? I sometimes ask. Why not me?

Like I said,
I would just be condemned to another useless shell to
store my soul.

Now here's how this existential funk has evolved:
      I had been trying to get out of my body for quite
some time now—without the help of drugs, I might add,
and I think I just uncovered the root cause of my drug
addiction, but I think I'll save that for another piece—but
now/
      here/
           today/
               on top of wanting to transcend, I've
been trying to cheat time————

To slow the clock

To speed up the clock

To stop the clock

To smash the clock

That kind of thing.
            But the thing is,
            as one event becomes another event,
            you will never, ever get back your

past. That's just the way it works. On
Tuesday, I sat in a car riding to a doctor's appointment, thinking how
strange, how mind-blowing, it is that
I'll be there soon and soon this moment will be history, lost to the
clutches of time.

Now it is Friday and I'm sitting in a coffee shop and in
five minutes I'll be doing something else. I'll be five
minutes older. That concept really blows my mind. Just
think about it. But do not yearn for the past because
that kind of thinking and wishing and wanting will get
you nowhere.

Anyway, I don't know the point of this; just to kill
time, I guess.
One day down, a lifetime of more to go....

Born in The Wrong Time

I remember when the Anti-Nowhere League played in
Providence, RI>>>>>>>>>>>>>>>
Great show...............................

I sang a duet with Animal, their singer——I got slugged
in the face from some tough-guy hardcore fag whose
punch overall lacked oomph—it forced my head backwards but that's about all it did, all because I split his lip
when I leaped from the stage—my elbow crashed into
his mouth and his lip let loose a thin line of blood that
dribbled down his chin—so fucking what?——and oh
yeah, Chuck and I crashed Gabby's dorm at some college
in Waltham, MA, we harassed her roommate who'd just
broken up with her boyfriend and was in her room crying over it, and Chuck and I laughed and we snuck into
the downstairs suite and stole beer and pizza from their
party earlier in the night I suppose///
Anyway the show, that's right....

I was out smoking a cigarette—Kristen threw a firework
my way, flung her lit butt at me and it swirled toward
my chin and kissed it and dropped to the ground, leaving me a peanut-sized burn on the right side—and I
threw one back that hit her in the chest and rolled down

into her bra and she howled—and I laughed——and then
I heard it———————
From inside came: **WE ARE THE LEAGUE!**, the intro to their
song "We're the League"—and with that I bolted with all
the drunken force I had and I was through the door and
the back of the bar and then the crowd—I shoved me a
path to the stage—and then I arrived and grasped the
edge and pulled myself up and rolled and stood and Animal passed me the mike and I took it of course and I was
howling as Animal wrapped an arm around my back and
I continued to howl through the whole first verse and
then the chorus and then passed back the mike to the
muscular singer wearing the outfit a caveman might
wear and leapt from the platform, jamming my elbow
into the hardcore fucker's mouth, and he whirled and
went after me and I turned, saw him directly in front of
me, and he spat:
                    YOU SPLIT MY LIP
I said, What? with a hand cupping my right ear///
What? I said. I can't hear you over the music—with a
jerk of my head I gestured toward the general direction
of the speakers looming over us.....................

              YOU SPLIT MY FUCKIN LIP

What? I said again—and his hand shot straight into me
and my face took the blow and my head snapped back
and then upright and I smirked and maybe even laughed
and this made him madder and he glared hard and spun
back around to face front///

Born in The Wrong Time

From behind me some Punk rock kid whispered in my ear: *Keep doing what you're doing, everyone here's got your back!*

See? that's what I call Punk rock unity for sure///

And after the show Kristen took her own car home and Chuck rode with me and Andy and we promised to give Gabby a ride back to her school even though she had ridden down with Kristen—guess her school was on our way and out of Kristen's///

We got there and got out and followed Gabby to her dorm to take a look inside—*Mwhahahahaha haha*—even though she specifically told us not to even though we kept saying yes we are even though she repeated no, don't even though she rode with us and we had all the right///
So it was like that—just like that——and we followed her across the parking lot——big bad Andy—Fat Andy—he followed close behind—lumbering like the nub he was—not too pleased about our plan to fuck shit up——it was always our plan, get used to it!———and we had arrived and followed Gabby through the door and up the steps, one thump at a time—our shoes and boots clattering against each step—and we were up and through the door and we were loud and overbearing I'm sure—until Gabby herself kicked us out and we slammed through the door a little pissed off by her demands—I mean who does she think she is?—and the whole time Andy is complaining: You guys were being total assholes————fuck you Andy, I said——yeah fuck you, Chuck repeated————and

—*BAM!!!*———

39

we were on the second floor—Gabby lived on the third—
—and on floor-number-two we cracked the door slightly
and stuck our heads into the dark apartment littered
with discarded pizza boxes and bottles of beer——and
the two of us—but not Andy of course—slunk through
the door like a couple greedy skunks and stole beer and
pizza————and then I got lost in the parking lot...........
——It's just how we rolled!

I shouted for Chuck and Andy——I turned in circles—
traversed the concrete in search of some sort of semblance———and there they were, I had arrived, and all
three of us stepped through the doors and—shaking his
head in dumb disapproval—Andy started the car and
pulled out of there///

——It's just how we rolled!

So   long story short—I feel like this is the wrong
generation for me—like if I lived 20 years earlier—30
years—I would have fit in just fine——I would have been
something—something more—something better———I'd
be a fuckin legend, for pete's sake....

The shit I did was the shit of legends———   Darby
Crash—for one——Sid Vicious—for another——Stiv Ba-
tors—Johnny Thunders—Johnny Rotten—Joe Strummer———————should I go on?

Just   what the fuck????

Born in The Wrong Time

I was born—I swear—in the wrong time, the wrong
generation, the wrong world————this world is not
right for me .... how many fuckin times
must I say that? should I spell it out for you///

I WAS BORN IN THE WRONG TIME

FUCK!!!

42

Irrelevant Battles

"You're too busy fighting your irrelevant battles / to see what's going on in your own backyard, / cuz some of us are having a hard, hard time."

— Patrik Fitzgerald

It's not good to agree for the sake of agreeing; it's not good to agree   period.... Because mindlessly saying okay causes even more problems than not; pampering is the behavior of the sick. Lifting one's ego, telling someone they're right all the time—wow, that's so unhealthy.

Me, I like to take the Devil's Advocate; I prefer to point out the fallacies of people's logic. I must fight, I will fight, I'm going to fight, just wait and see—cuz my rhetoric is better than yours.

But then,   What for? I realize now.

Some people are too set in their ways to see where their argument breaks, too self-righteous I like to say———
the master of rhetoric, the King of the Debate, can see both sides of any argument, can smell their own shit from miles away.

Jeremy Void

Take control of your own life:

                    Recognize where you're wrong.

I want to show others their own shit, point it out to them
so that they can see where they need improvement.
Say, Look, you stink, your logic stinks. But sometimes
nothing I say is strong enough to change said person's
mind.
So I ask myself,   What for?

I don't really give a shit how far you're able to piss. And
I'm certainly not going to try my hand at pissing any
farther.   It's just not worth my time.
                That kind of battle is so irrelevant.
I've got more important wars to fight, more important
battles to pick.
My friend is currently detoxing from heroin, and I'm
giving him a hand, giving him a chance at a better life.

So,   sometimes it's just not worth it.
                Don't try and convince a Catholic that there
                    is no God;
                don't attempt to tell an Atheist that there is.
                      How the hell
                    can they be so sure?
                        anyway

They're too stubborn and immature.   Look, I'm not
exactly sure of anything in the end myself, and I don't
exactly pretend that I am.
Take everything you hear with a grain of salt.

Born in The Wrong Time

So,   sometimes I just keep my mouth shut. Don't partake in an argument with a moron, unless you yourself are willing to be treated like one. You will be denied, rejected, kicked to the curb, and your point will be lost because said idiot is just not willing to see another side but their own.

"You don't know what you're talking about."

"Is that a joke?"

"That's the stupidest thing I've ever heard."

"Don't even go there."

                    ... lesson learned ...

My Older Brother's Wedding

Wednesday night I got really depressed. Nobody commented on or even LIKEd my last five posts on Facebook, and this fact pushed me spiraling and flailing off the edge and into a dark and desolate place. I know, it sounds like a stupid reason to get all bent out of shape, but that's not the real reason, just the catalyst that set the wheels of hopelessness into motion.

First of all, my younger sister, Elana, got married a month ago, and my older brother, Daniel, was to get married in just a few days. (I was scheduled to fly down to Boston the following day.) This means everyone in my immediate family would soon be married. Kristen, who I'd always felt was perfect for me—and she'd even said so herself—and I had broken up maybe a month before Elana's wedding.
So that leaves me hopelessly and utterly alone.

Second of all, I seem to have writer's block; I can't seem to write anything worth a damn as of lately.

These two facts—my siblings getting married and my writer's block—plus the upcoming move to Boston, which I assume adds a whole other level of stress to my life, have been boiling up inside me, like a steaming hot pot of angst, and on Wednesday night the stew, roiling and bubbling and fizzing, rose to the top of the pot and spilled over.

I told my friend Molly, who was to accompany me to Daniel's wedding—as a friend and only as a friend—that I was not in fact going, I deactivated my Facebook account, and as the feelings of self-pity festered inside I sprang up to my feet and bashed my laptop on the ground, picked it up off the floor and bashed it again and again until it was just a measly heap of junk.

On Thursday I slept all day. I didn't answer the phone for anyone. My caseworker came by to check on me a couple of times, but I just told him everything was fine and went back to sleep.

When I fall into these states I usually sleep for a few days, then get up and brush myself off like it never happened. But this time it only took one day to recover. Too bad I forget this fact amid these bouts, because now I'm out a computer.

Come Friday morning I phoned my dad, we talked for a bit about what had happened, and I agreed to fly down to Boston later that day, at four-thirty PM. I met with my caseworker and my therapist and they both agreed that that was fine.

So I got to the airport at about four-o'clock, checked in, took a Klonopin (the doctor prescribed four for the duration of the weekend, no more than two a day), and sat down and waited for my flight. Since I don't take Klonopin regularly anymore, the pill hit hard and the flight itself felt as if it only took fifteen minutes before the plane touched down at Logan Airport.

I missed the rehearsal and made it about an hour late for the party in my parents' backyard. I saw cousins and aunts and uncles, and others with whom I was not yet acquainted. I went to say hi to Sabrina, my brother's fiancé, but said hi to the wrong girl. (Sabrina is Chinese, and I feel that all Chinese look the same, though they probably feel the same about us.)

The following day, Saturday, the day of the wedding, I went and got a haircut, showered, and took the Green Line to Park Street, where I met up with Molly, who looked absolutely stunning. We said hi, hugged, and then hopped on the Green Line back to Newton.

The wedding was at the DeCordova Museum in Lincoln, MA. Before I had to meet up with Daniel, Sabrina, and the rest of the wedding party, Molly and I had half an hour to ourselves to just roam the grounds. I took some really great pictures of her, and of us.

Then my brother called and I had to go meet the wedding party for photos. I actually had fun this time; the photographers were a lot more laid back than the ones at Elana's wedding. They got a picture of me and Daniel after I unexpectedly hopped on his back.

The wedding itself was boring. I stood in back holding the hupa, or whatever it's called. I saw Molly weaving

her way around snapping pictures of the marriage. It
ended with my brother Daniel stamping his foot on a
glass bottle, but not hard enough, as he had to stamp it a
second time.

The crowd rose up and spilled out of there, conjuring in
the museum, where drinks were served, hors d'oeuvre
floated atop the hands of waiters and waitresses, and
Molly and I slipped away to look at the exhibits. There
was one exhibit I particularly liked, where the artist had
played around with words to really create a visceral
experience for the viewer. It kind of reminded me of
my own visual art.

This segment of the evening passed rather quick, and
the crowd was directed to reassemble in a tent outside
of the museum. The wedding party, by order of the DJ,
had to form a line inside the museum proper, in pairs—
except for me, as I was grouped with my sister and her
husband Mike. The DJ waved his hand, and someone who
stood in front beckoned each pair, one by one, to leave
the museum and stride into the tent.
As the pairs crossed the threshold, the DJ announced
their names, and the whole tent exploded with cheers, as
though we were all basketball players stepping out onto
the court before a game.

Before my group of three was beckoned forward, Elana
and Mike and I frantically asked the pair before us if
they were going to do anything special upon entering
the tent, and they said they weren't sure. I suggested we
all do backflips upon entering. Neither Mike nor Elana
was game for that, so instead I just strolled in with my

left arm looped through Elana's right, Mike's right through her left. I held up this wooden stick I had found, which had pink wooden lips on its tip, as if the lips were my own, and as I crossed the threshold, I tossed it at the crowd, though it didn't go very far.

I found a seat beside Molly and the food was served. The first course was something weird, some sort of strange salad, and I gave mine to Molly. The second course was brisket, which was really good.

During dinner Molly said she'd crash with me at my parents' house because she didn't want to leave on the ten PM shuttle. I found my parents and asked if that was okay, and they said it was fine.

Then the party really got going. I have to give it up for the DJ, for he really knew how to rile a crowd. The dance floor was packed, everyone was dancing, even I danced, and if Molly wasn't there, I probably wouldn't have. She and I danced together, we danced with others, I jumped on my brother's back again, he struggled to keep me afloat, and everyone moved out of the way when I lifted Molly horizontally on my shoulder and spun her around and around. I probably danced for four hours straight, with the occasional cigarette break. Molly doesn't smoke, so no wonder she was so tired by the end of the night and just wanted to go home.

We left the tent and headed up to the room designated for the wedding party at about eleven-thirty. Shortly after midnight we left with my parents, and my mom called a cab for Molly. The cab was already at my parents' house waiting when we got there. I walked Molly to the cab, said thanks for coming, gave her a hug, and waved as the cab pulled out.

In my parents' basement now, I texted her: *Hey, I just wanna reiterate that I really appreciate you coming with me because, like I said, I've been kinda depressed as of lately, and I had a lot of fun with you tonight. And I hope you feel better.*

She wrote back: *Aww good I hope I made you feel better.*

And: *You are a good friend.*

I woke up the following morning at eight, texted her to let me know if she wanted to go to the Chinese Banquet, and fell back asleep until five PM. Apparently, according to her return text, she slept in too.

Prejudgments

If you do NOT know me, please do not PRETEND that you know me. This includes all those who've met me only once or twice in their miserable lives. And it especially includes if you've gotta a good read on me, because if you have to get a read on me, then chances are you do not know me well enough to make an accurate assessment.

**   ⧖   **

I was talking to an old friend tonight, who showed up at my doorstep to buy a book—well, sort of. He told me that when we used to hang out he had a therapist who suggested he not hang out with me anymore because, she said, I'm a bad influence on him.

This girl (A) blew me one night in my living room, and then came a series of thumps on my window, and when I pushed the shade to the side I saw it was this other girl (B) who lived above me, and she knew the topless girl in my living room, and the girl who lived above me stood outside my window waving an angry fist in the direction of me.

I sat there while girl A scurried out my door and met
girl B on the front yard, and I watched while the two
girls screamed at one another, and moments later girl A
stormed back inside and said girl B claimed I was a bad
influence and she shouldn't hang out with me anymore.

The friend I spoke to last night told me he of course
disobeyed his therapist by hanging out with me. I asked
who she was, what her name was, and he told me somebody by the name of M------, and then I asked how she
knew me, and he said she knew all the people from the
rooms—all the people from AA.
sounds like a breach of anonymity if you ask me
(a therapist of all people, someone being paid to help
you)

There's this halfway house down the street from where
I live called the Grace House, and I know all those who
live there are judging me, saying I'm not sober even
though I claim to be, but then again, who are they? and
why are their thoughts and judgments so important that
I should let it bother me at all?
I was with a friend not affiliated with AA, and he and I
were on our way to Pub 42 because I go there weekly to
read at the open-mikes, but not to drink because I don't
do that anymore; and as we walked past the Grace House
my friend made a phone call and said into his phone
that we're on our way to Pub 42—right in front of a clus-
ter of smokers lingering out on the front porch of the
Grace House—and I could imagine then all the reactions
of those sitting out on the front porch of the Grace
House smoking butts and listening in because there were
quite a few of them out there at that very moment, and

Prejudgments

at first I admit I stumbled a bit which is a direct result
of my anxiety, but then the more I thought about it, a
smile started to form on my face, drawn from ear to
ear, getting wider and more gleeful, and soon enough
even laughter started to bubble up from my gut,
glimmering from deep down inside me.
        (because I laugh when I do something foolish or when
                something foolish is done to me—like something
        unavoidable that would make others shriek and maybe
                        think I'm a freak)

The friend who I saw earlier tonight, he himself used to
live at the Grace House, back when the two of us hung
out more often, and he told me about all the crap they
used to say about me, about how they used to hate me
for no other reason than the fact that I was me, and it's
things like that that they detest for some reason.
                i.e. people who don't know me claiming I'm a bad
                                                influence

I don't really get why others judge people they don't
know. Don't get me wrong, I'm not against judging people
because making judgments is part of the human condi-
tion, in that we have to judge to survive; if we ever want
to get ahead, we must make assessments about others.
But why judge someone or something we know nothing
about?
Why talk intellectually about a subject we don't understand ourselves?
It's like what Socrates said: Those who admit they know
nothing are the smartest of us all.
        (though I know those aren't the exact words that he
                                used)

I had a girlfriend who was so stubborn it drove me crazy to talk to her, and being so stubborn like that she was convinced she was right all the time, and she never even thought it possible that she could be wrong and the opposition could be right.

The only virtue that I value is open-mindedness because without it you are ignorant and ignorance is something that I strive against.

When I was younger I spoke at length with that aforementioned stubborn girlfriend of mine saying how I wished I was an animal, how I wished to sorely rely on my instinct and not my intellect, and she asked me why because I'm fairly intelligent even though I play it off like I'm not, and so why would I want to resort to that level?
But that's the thing about being an animal. You know nothing else, and by virtue of knowing nothing else you simply don't care either way.
              it's just funny how things change over time....

Interpreting Poetry

In Dimensions of Freedom at CCV we learned how to read
poetry.
               HOW TO READ POETRY
               are you kidding me?

You should not have to learn how to read it. If it doesn't
          come automatically it's not worth reading, I think.
Or maybe that's not true....
Maybe what makes it good is its cerebral aspect. Maybe
          the fact that you have to stop and think about it is
          what makes a good poem good. Maybe.
I don't know....
If the poem is unreadable then the meaning is lost and
the reader's connection to the poem wasn't meant to be.
                              Maybe...................

YOU CANNOT LEARN HOW TO READ
               poetry
any more than you can throw it....

BECAUSE THE NATURE OF EDUCATION IS
               standardization
AND if it has to be taught then the purpose is lost....

Jeremy Void

You cannot teach a writer how to write!
You cannot teach an artist how to paint or draw!
Nor can a photographer learn how to snap shots of the
    world!

It must come from inside....
        education only standardizes
        and art cannot be standardized unless
        it's generic and boring ....
        commercialized crap/// Teachers teach you

how to fall in line, how to follow the rules,
how to read poetry the way they deem fit.
                See what I'm getting at here?

Reading poetry cannot be taught anymore than
viewing art can be taught....

There is no methodology to such a thing, I don't care
what they say, I don't care how convincing they are or
how confusing the piece of art is to interpret—it cannot
be taught

although that's not to say there aren't strategies for
dissecting a poem, but the strategies must come from
inside you, they must be genuinely yours or the meaning will be lost to you—
the more you read poetry the easier it is to understand,
and that cannot be taught   PERIOD

So save your breath next time you think about teaching
someone the insider secrets of how to dissect a poem!
It's just not gonna work.

Johntober Fest 3

From the Beginning:

When I was a kid going to shows
was what I lived for—getting
knocked around in the pit while a
deafening roar splintered the
speakers, ripping through the venue
one thrashing power cord after an-
other, it could not be beat. They say
you drink to forget—me, I pogoed to
forget, I slammed with no regrets,
jamming the rotten memory of that
pretentious cunt rejecting me last
week right out of my head cuz
when I was spinning, kicking, swing-
ing, crashing into others who were
doing virtually the same, nothing
else mattered to me.

I kicked and bobbed, I swung
and hopped, moving like a dazzling,
haphazard, flittering projectile of
pure furry and force to the music
that reverberated through the
hall—some would scurry out of my

*way, while others would throw
themselves right into me.*
     *——For those who know
nothing of Punk rock, don't think of
this as just another violent sport
like football or lacrosse or hockey,
cuz it's really not. To us it's just
fun and games, there are no win-
ners, there are no losers, people
rarely get hurt in the pit too, and if
one of our comrades gets knocked
down a volley of hands will instantly surge out as the onlookers
desperately grasp for the fallen sol-
dier and help him/her to his/her
feet.*

**A Day
in the Life
of a Punk.**

**   ⏳   **

Saturday night I went to a show called Johntober Fest 3,
located in Stockbridge, VT. All I know of the town is that
everyone carries a gun, that much is certain.

At about 4:30 PM, expecting a call from Josh to tell me he
was on his way, I sat on my couch trying to keep my
head afloat as it drifted downward and my lights
momentarily ebbed, but I caught myself and pushed my
head back up each time// You see, I got no sleep the
previous night, so you bet I was exhausted.

I started to hallucinate too.
Like the monster that crawled
out of my dresser drawer—it
was made of clothing. Or the
few times I felt like I was float-
ing and nearly panicked when I
couldn't feel the couch beneath
me; I flailed my arms and
gasped but quickly found that
the couch was still beneath
me—thank God.

At roughly 4:45 Josh called and said he was leaving now,
he'd be there in ten minutes; I said okay and grabbed my
stuff and hurried out the door and met him on the
street.
Instead of his girlfriend coming with us it was Pete. On
the drive I read the two of them "A Bag Full of God,"
which killed the majority of the time in the car, leaving
a good fifteen minutes left.

On the final stretch of highway, Josh and Pete and I
traversed the road, going back and forth in search of
some semblance to where we were heading—nothing; we
were lost.

The three things we knew:
1. To get to the show you had to climb a steep hill.
2. There would be a skateboard truck flipped on its
   side at the bottom of said hill.
3. There was a restaurant, whose name I can't
   remember, a block away.

We saw the restaurant and pulled over at the bottom of a steep hill that wound its way into the woods. But there was no skateboard truck flipped on its side. But still— this must be the right place, we decided, and since we had no cellphone service here, there was no turning back, this was our decision.

We got out of the car and figured we'd climb the hill to scope how long of a hike it was before unloading the gear, although I brought my backpack up with me so I had more free hands to help carry the equipment when the time came.
Pete and Josh seemed to have climbed the hill no prob- lem. I saw them reach the top, not the least bit winded, tiny silhouettes against the sunny backdrop; but me, I was only halfway up and I was panting raggedly—a sure sign that I have to hit the gym sometime soon. Plus, I had two bags full of books hanging off of me, which surely didn't help me out much.

I arrived at the top of the hill, where a puzzled Josh and a baffled Pete stood panning the site with quizzical eyes. We stood in a near-empty field, with a haphazard trailer park set-up to our left and on our right was just an open field, with what looked like a spot for a bon fire in the distance. I sat down at the picnic table to catch my breath as Josh continued up the hill and Pete branched out in a different direction.
The strange thing was, there was supposed to be a skate park here, I thought to myself, just as a white pickup truck ascended the steep incline and slowed to a stop in the field.

You think that might be John, I shouted, my voice scattering in the emptiness to catch up with both Josh and Pete. I looked the way Pete had gone and I saw him hurrying back toward me, and up the way Josh had gone and he was descending the stretch of hill he had just climbed. They both met me in the field.
The door of the pickup truck popped open, and the man who came out was neither John nor anyone else we were familiar with, but a disgruntled, red-faced old man carrying in his right hand a large bronze revolver.

Shit!

The guy shouted at us, What are you doing on my property?
We're lost, Josh said.
Show me your Goddamned IDs, he barked at us.

Josh and I complied right away, but Pete stood his ground, saying in a somewhat defiant tone, On whose authority?

On the authority of the guy whose property you're on. You're lucky I don't call the cops.

A friendly pat on Pete's chest by me told him to stop dicking around.

(Later, I would explain to him that it's not about rights and freedom, but the fact that this guy just came home to see

us three wander-
ing around his
property and he
didn't know what
to think. But he
let us go, only be-
cause we so easily
complied. We com-
plied with his de-
mands, and then
he let us explain,
and then we were
off the hook—just
like that.)

The old man eventually let us go, having opened the
floor for an explanation, and Josh did the explaining,
and as we walked away, the guy shouted, Sorry to
frighten you guys with the gun.

Either Pete or Josh shouted back, Don't you think
the gun was unnecessary.

Everyone around here's got a gun.

We don't, said Josh, and down the hill we went, on
shaking legs that made the descent rather difficult.

Soon after, we found the place, and the anxiety shared
between the three of us had subsided, and we parked, got
out, and said hi, and people were like:

You guys got a gun pulled on you?
and I was like:

Yeah, cuz we're more badass than you,

and then everybody laughed, and it felt good to be out of harm's way, in the good company of friends, waiting for the show to start.

Immediately this girl named Erica showed us around: the skate park, mostly. The place was really sick.
We were some of the first people to arrive since we had all the gear: the PA, etc.

We squandered the property, and I drank Monsters while everyone else drank beer and whiskey and smoked weed.

At 7:30 the show started. Middle Son was up first. It was funny cuz you couldn't see their faces at all because the tent blocked our view of them—except when Hunter ducked beneath the tent and joined the crowd as he thrashed the guitar and wobbled and hopped and swayed and staggered, the guitar in his hands like a battle axe as he prepared himself for war.

Then he climbed back onstage and disappeared behind the tent again to be a faceless musician.

The next performer wasn't exactly a band, but a stand-up comedian named Richard Bowen, who carried around some sort of portable speaker box attached to a microphone (which I so have to get). His jokes were hysterical, and later he told me he gets his inspiration from thinking too much—I can totally relate....

Then I went and read,

and one more band played, though only a few seemed to give a shit at that point. It was amazing, the normal singer of that band had to get his vocal cords removed from screaming too much. That's one of my worst fears: NO MORE PERFORMING!

Near the skate park the fire raged, and people stood around in its flaming warmth as skaters skated and drunk Punks conversed.

> Throughout the evening I unloaded all my samplers. Too bad I didn't sell a book though. I did donate *An Art Form* to one of the bands, gave Champion John a copy of *Derelict America* for his birthday, and gave Richard Bowen a copy of *Just a Kid*, since I enjoyed his stand-up and thought he'd enjoy my writing (I was to give him my last sampler, but for a while I couldn't find him and, thinking he had left, I gave it to someone else, so I didn't have any samplers left to give him and so I gave him *Just a Kid*.)

All and all, for being the only sober person there, I'd say I had a great time. People were amazed that, what with my history with drugs, I could stay sober through it all, and I told them it was a result of my attending AA and one of the promises is to be rid of the desire to drink and/or do drugs.

For the drive home we picked up a fourth passenger—David—and he sat barely awake in the passenger seat and I sat beside a passed-out Pete in the back, and the only noise in the car on the ride home were the rare words Josh and I exchanged. I know, for me, I felt wired, even though I didn't sleep the previous night. I felt good and wired, and
when I got home I passed out in the next hour.

68

Where's My Life-Second-to-None?

In AA, I frequently hear, *I've got a life second to none.* Which I'm starting to think is crap. I'm starting to wonder if what they mean by that is, people in AA have actually in fact learned to accept their lives as it is, because, after all, it could be so much worst; they could be in jails, institutions, or, worst, dead.

Well, that's not what I want for myself: to just accept life for what it is. I want my life to actually get *better*. I want to get out of this mess.

I know it sounds like a selfish thing to say, because if that's truly the case, then I must only be doing good things for others so as to secure the outcome. *You are just a means to an end,* is what I must be thinking. But it's not what I'm thinking.

For the past few months I've had *no* hope that life will ever get better. None. Yet I continue to help, continue to go out of my way for the sake of others—and doing good things doesn't always feel good, internally or externally; I don't care what they say. It's not fun. Never was, and never will be.

But still I continue to help, continue to reach my hand out to others. Why? Because it's the right thing to do; because it's my duty as a human being. And yes, sometimes my motives are mixed up, but that's only because I have an ailment shared by everyone—which means **you!**

Well, anyway, I want my life to get better; not just to accept my limitations as such.

I shared this issue at the AA meeting, and mostly what I've heard is that true happiness doesn't come from materials, it comes from spirituality. Just have faith, and you will be taken care of. Which doesn't mean you'll get a fancy car, a big house, a beautiful wife, or even be a *best-selling author*, one person said specifically. Just be happy that you're not drunk and in a ditch; be happy that you're not Chuck, because *his* life is a mess. Sure, he's got more in his life than I have in my life, material-wise, but he has no spirituality; he's spiritually bank-rupt.

Be grateful. Grateful. Grateful grateful grateful. Gratitude. To deal with life on life's terms, is what AA teaches. It's all AA teaches.
On that note, I'm closing the notebook and throwing away my Styrofoam cup and sneaking out of the meeting early, because I have an appointment at one.

At the Zen Garden

At the Zen Garden in Poultney, VT, right now. The view here is beautiful, is what they tell me. But to me it's rather mundane, which is why I'm writing rather than marveling at the magnificently big opening that shows trees and ferns and open fields and rocky cliffs, et cetera et cetera—————————
  Yawn!
Anyway, it's freezing out. Seems like a weird place to go in this weather, but that's where everyone else wanted to go so I guess it's something to do for now. A change of scenery, I guess.

       I never wrote about my last trip to Boston. I started writing about it a few times, but each time I didn't finish. Hopefully I'll finish it this time. I mean, I do have some time to kill.

       So here I go:

My AA sponsor, Robert, and his family happened to be going down to the Cape on Friday, September 5th, so I hitched a ride with them down to Boston. They dropped me off at my parents' house in Newton, MA, that night.

In the car, NPR played on the radio. There was an interview with Chris Archangel, or Chris Angel, or Chris Something or Another. I think that's the magician with his own TV show, and he does stuff like levitate, although on the radio the interviewer introduced him as a contemporary artist. So maybe I'm thinking of someone else.

Anyway, he's coming out with a book; that was the point of the broadcast: to promote his new book. He's calling the book *Fiction,* for irony's sake. The book he wrote—or moreover, didn't write—is supposed to be a collection of other's people's tweets. I don't use Twitter, so I didn't actually know this. Apparently it's common practice on Twitter to say you're working on a novel—— or moreover, to *claim* you're working on a novel. This artist, Chris Archangel or Chris Angel or something like that, has drawn the conclusion that most of these claims are false, that people just want to seem deep or esoteric or something; so this "novel" of his, which he did not actually write, is supposed to be a satirical look at society, he says—what a joke!
Honestly, I think it's an amazing idea, I really do; it's really creative and artistic. But that's all it is: *an idea.* A skilled novelist would take that *idea* and twist it into an actual novel. I guess that's the difference between art and literature, for art—or should I say visual art—is nothing but an idea, a foundation, something to base a story around, whereas literature is exploratory, in that it takes ideas and explores them; it delves beyond the surface.
In an interview by Stephen King, he says he writes to satisfy curiosity.

At the Zen Garden

So, I arrived at my parents' house late Friday night and pretty much went to sleep soon after.

Come Saturday I went clothes shopping. Last time I went to Boston, when I flew back, the airline had lost just about all my clothing. I went down there with a large laundry bag filled with almost all my clothing, and when I got off the plane, arriving back in Rutland, VT, it was gone. After three days of pestering the airline they finally said it was gone for good. So on Saturday I went clothes shopping with my dad; I didn't get much though, just enough to get me through the next few days—and until the airline sends me the reimbursement check, which they will do, I am certain of that.

Sunday I went to a show in Harvard Square, at a place called Follow the Honey. Which was basically the main reason for my visit. Molly wanted me to go with her. Said I'd like the place, and the people; so I arranged to go....

Before the show I met up with Skylar and his girl-friend in Harvard Square. In my short story "Stink-Box," the main character, Derek Defect, gets arrested with a younger guy because he sets his beer in between him and the younger guy, and when the cops come they assume the beer belongs to the younger guy and Derek gave it to him.
The younger guy is Skylar.

> Back when I lived in Boston and hung out with Skylar more regularly, Chuck and I treated him like

73

dirt, probably because he
was younger and he
made for an easy target;
and because when I was
his age the older kids
had hazed me too, so I
was only passing off the
torch, so to speak.
But now, I'm a changed man.
Really I am<<<<<<<<<<<<<<<<<<<<<<<<<
I don't particularly feel bad for my
past transgressions, but I do know
they were wrong and nobody deserves to be treated the way I treated
him; if anything, I treated him worst
than the bastards had treated me.
- We made him drink dog piss.
- Outside a show Fink and I
  smashed a trashcan over his
  head.
(His dad pulled up in the parking lot just as we did it,
and when Chuck and I hopped in the backseat hoping to
hitch a ride with him back to Newton, his dad just looked
at us and said, frighteningly calm, Get out!)

- Skylar showed up in Harvard
  Square that day with a deep
  welt on his forehead and told
  me it was from when I threw
  him head-first into a dish-
  washer at some house party.
So I did apologize to him when I saw him. Like I said, I
don't particularly feel bad about what I'd done but I

know quite well that my actions were wrong; so I did the mature thing and apologized.

He said he really appreciated it, and I could tell from his reaction that he really *really* appreciated it.

Also:

- I saw JP in Harvard Square too (he was the original drummer of my old band Lethal Erection)
- I bought a book on meditation from an actual monk for four dollars
- I went for a drive around Central Square with Skylar and his girlfriend.

They swung me back to the Pit, where I got out and went to meet up with Molly.

Before the show she and I stopped and got Mexican food, of which I wasn't particularly fond myself.

Lately my appetite has been little to none.

So, the show was at a place called Follow the Honey. When we got there, there was a man and woman onstage. The man sang while the woman played acoustic guitar. It was a very small crowd. First thing when I got there, I asked someone who I would talk to about me reading a poem. The man I asked said I wanted to talk to the man onstage. Which is what I did. When he and the woman finished their set, I approached him with my question, and he said yes. He said I could read while the next band was setting up.

Which is what I figured he'd say.

I read "To the Girl I Love," and most of them, if not all,
seemed to love it. I could tell at first they didn't know
what to make of it
because the first two lines are:

*"My erect penis sticks up and points to the one I love.
Her crisp nipples jut out and lock onto my swollen heart."*

I picked that one because it's
shocking and I needed something that would hook their
attentions right away.

I left the show before it ended though. I wasn't feeling
so well later in the night. Mostly I was just feeling awkward and out of place—these were all hippies and I was
this rough-looking Punk rocker, so yeah I was a bit out
of place.
On the train back to Newton I wrote this on
Facebook: *I'm staring at my phone trying to figure out how to
express my deepest feelings, but I can't because I'm
just so blank tonight; that or I think I forgot how to
feel a long time ago. I heard someone say, "I wanna
cry but I don't know how," and I think that just about
says it all.*
Which basically sums it up. Not that I have no feelings,
because I do; but I can't seem to identify them all the
time. I know *anger* and *hate* very well—even though I
don't consider *hate* an emotion—and I know *sadness* and
what *jaded* feels like; but when it comes to digging beyond the surface of said emotions, I'm lost—it's like the
shovel hits a stone and won't go any deeper into the dirt.
Like a wall of stones blocks any attempt at entering my
heart. Basically, I don't know what makes me tick. My

old poetry used to just be angry nonsense. Because I could never seem to get beyond the surface of my initial feelings.

So I went back to my parents' house. On the train I got a text from Molly asking if I was all right.
I said I was fine/
I said I was just tired/

I lied to her, but then, I didn't exactly know how to tell the truth, now, did I?

** **

Presently it's five AM on a Saturday, one week after I wrote everything above, and two weeks after my latest trip to Boston. But I haven't finished the telling of my weekend yet.

So here I go:

My last day before I flew back, I went to Panera Bread in the afternoon. In their dining room, there was a small section in the back that was somewhat secluded from the rest of the diners. Sitting in that section was only an older gentleman who was quietly reading the newspaper.

So I took a seat there, pulled out my book, and started reading.
Ten minutes later a group of six or seven rambunctious middle-aged women entered. They were so freaking loud. The first thing they did upon entering was complain about the place—about how it was too hot, about how it was too bright, to name a few.

Jeremy Void

They even brought in the manager, and he said they
could close the shades if they wanted to. I was reading,
for fuck's sake, and it's kind of hard to read in the dark.
Plus, I don't exactly want glasses any time soon, so I keep
the lights on when I read.
They didn't even notice me there, it seemed, until one
lady pointed at me and said, Oh he's just trying to relax—*you got that right!*
Another woman said, It's okay, this is just how women
our age act.

Can you believe that shit????

The One That Got Away
A Lewd Recount of Events

The other day a friend says to me he wants to start writing more. He says, Where do you get your ideas from?

At first I say, I don't know.
>> But then I told him, Just start from the top
and the rest will flow right out of
you————
So where do I begin?

Well, for starters<<<< I just got back from the bar about two hours ago, and just now, with my pants around my ankles, my hard dick sticking out, and a big-titted gal getting plowed on my computer screen, I find myself thinking, *What gives????*   I'm always seeing these average-looking guys—guys who I'm definitely smarter than, definitely hotter than; guys who I blow so far out of the water it's not even funny—with these gorgeous girls hanging off them. I mean, *What the hell gives?* Like, dirty Punk kids with hot, model-like preppy girls, clean and neat-looking—girls who don't look like the type to be dating this specific breed of cretin. Scruffy, long-haired metalheads with big-titted, blond-haired chicks. Dirty,

fat dudes with these gorgeous tens around their necks
that I could never see myself getting with—ever.

> First of all, one of
> my biggest follies
> has always been
> the tendency to
> compare myself to
> others.

Like, I've been with a few "normal"-looking girls in my
lifetime, and it's always been something special to me,
cuz to me they're exotic, they're the forbidden fruit
which the snake in my pants is always trying to chide
me into biting. Trust me, I do know what they taste
like—I really do

> they taste as sweet
> as vice....

But it just doesn't seem fair to think that mostly they've
shunned me all my life.

> But don't get me
> wrong, I do love
> Kristen, and I love
> all the other girl-
> friends I've ever
> had, and also all
> the other alterna-
> tive lovers that
> have been fortu-
> nate enough to
> taste my cock.

Maybe I'm only saying this because I'm lonely right
now—and I'm definitely only saying it cuz I'm jealous; I

definitely have a tendency to covet my neighbor's wives, as I've said, when I've probably felt more pussy than they have in their own lives.

After a show Lethal Erection played I was talking to my friend Derek who stood there with his hot, preppy girl-friend, and Kristen might have been standing there too, who knows?—Derek was the first one to say I was just like Darby Crash, after he went and read *Lexicon Devil* (I always wonder what happened to that kid)—and I was complaining that my life was so shitty, I wanted to die, boo hoo, pour me, cry me a fucking river, *I mean come on, get over yourself now!*—you know what I'm talking about—and he looked me square in the eye and said, *Dude, you're life is so good, you're dating Kristen*———and that really made me think about things....

       So many guys I knew have had a crush on her, and I was the one who ended up with her———*her!* of all people....

            (How's that for fair? I still don't think I deserved a girl like that.)

       And yet they—the other guys I see around from time to time—got the blond-haired, good-looking chicks—not that Kristen isn't good-looking, because she is absolutely beautiful, she is really one of a kind and she was all mine. Kristen is cool as hell and smart and pretty and fun fun fun——and I mean *fun!*—SO MUCH FUN!!!   She was the whole package.   So what, I didn't end up with the traditional looker, the neat girls who smell just as sweet—cuz I ended

up with a girl who was cool with me doing
cocaine and smoking crack and shooting it
too, and she did it right there with me,
and—*this is the best part*—she danced in the
moshpit (show me a preppy girl who would
do that) and she was the only girl to dance
in there too——well, her and her best friend
Gabby were the only ones to dance in
there——and they looked so hot as they
failed and slammed together, and you bet I
joined right in, and sometimes it would only
be us three dancing as the crowd stood
around us.

So I guess I *was* lucky.   We always covet the things
we don't got—or at least I do.   I don't know what your
girlfriend tastes like and it drives me crazy not knowing,
so I sit alone in my apartment after the open-mike at
the Center Street Alley, and I speculate and I fantasize
and I rub myself until a white, gooey substance spurts
out of me, and then I remember that I had the pleasure
of tasting a goddess; not you, but *me*—a girl all my good
friends sought after, a girl who chose me me me in the
end—*God knows why!*—and I couldn't handle her love, and I
simply don't deserve her anyway; so she's gone now and
I'm all alone with only a hand for company. There's
worst company to have I guess.

She's definitely the one that got away, and I hate to say it
but she ruined me because now the thought of being with
another girls frightens the hell out of me and I would just
as well curl up in a ball and hide before ... you know ... getting with a ten, anyway. So why let it worry me at all?

Fear of Losing It

"The only fear I have left is the fear of not being able to create."

— Marylyn Manson

I'm horrified right now
cuz for so long I have been on a roll. It was like my
muse was doing speed, sending me signals that put me in
a trance for me to pound out yet another poem/// One
more to add to my collection—
but it seems now like my writing has become too scat-
tered, it seems now like I'm running out of ideas and I've
been forcing the words to come out of me. But you can't
force it—or at least I can't———you've just gotta let them
roll out of your mind with ease. You've gotta treat your
creativity with tender care, you've gotta nurture it,
nurse it to life, like a pet cat.... If you abuse it
you will lose it....

Period!

I heard someone say at an AA meeting today that it isn't
in her nature to do things correctly. When faced with an
opportunity she abuses the shit out of it and thus loses
it. That's so me.

Jeremy Void

Everything I've been given, every opportunity offered,
every chance for advancement, every gift to rid me of
my wretched circumstances, I rode straight to the
ground....

Gimme a chance, a chance
is all I need to show you
          just how much of a fuckup
          I really am
I mean I got high off oxygen....

Anyway, that's aside the point.

What I'm getting at here is I abused my creative side for
the past year, I rode it full-throttle, and squeezed the
last bit of life right out of it   and now it's fading
away like rising bubbles, dissipating as fate grabs it and
sends it on its way....

I'm horrified right now>>>
You wanna know what drives this fear?
For so long I'd been having a blast. My muse and I had
become good friends—best friends in fact—and I thought
it would never end, but
one's muse is a tricky thing. It comes and goes as it
pleases, it's got a mind of its own, and if you nurture it,
keep it happy as you paint or draw or write or snap pictures of the insane world we live in, it might stick
around for longer, but then

who knows?

It's a tricky thing.

Fear of Losing It

I'm not even sure where the term "muse" comes from,
what exactly it means, nor do I really care. It just is
what it is, and it was   what it was——   the past is
set in stone and can't be changed by anyone....
Sure, the future can be doctored by your present decisions plus circumstances ... but it's still   quite
unpredictable....

I was writing so much, but now
it's over
that sensation of creating
is fading away from me.
I wrestle to get it back
I struggle to hold on
and squeeze out all the last little drops of
creativity onto the page....

But It's No Use——

I might as well give up now. I might as well let go of the
hope that soon I will be on a roll again   just like before
just like yesterday
and the day before

but hope only serves one purpose :: :: :: to cause one suf-
fering.

So I let go of this dream, of this fabrication that one day
I will be a star, that one day I will have a best seller, be a
household name, a name you can't forget because **Jeremy**

Jeremy Void

Void will be engrained in the public eye, hammered into
the back of people's minds. That's my dream, that's my
quest, but if this muse abandons me I will be one step
farther from my overall goal.
I will be back where I started, just another nobody
with a bad case of writer's block....

I always said writer's block was
a cop out....   an excuse so that
you don't have to put the pedal
to the grindstone, so that you don't have to write....

I'm horrified right now,,,,,   did I mention that?

My Cat Richie Dagger

A few years ago I was living in a halfway house we call
Royce St. because it sits right on Royce St. I was still
amid my rebellious ways back then, and anger and
frustration brooded deep within my soul. I was pissed,
and rightfully so.
So I would run away/
I would hitchhike to Burlington,

         and then ...

            well, that was
            about as far as I
            got in the planning
            of all this//

So there you have it.
After all the bedtime meds were dished out and everybody was fast asleep, including Bev, the woman who
worked on weekends, who stayed overnight in the spare
room down in the basement,

            (Royce St. came complete with
            a live-in staff and at the time I
            believe it was Elizabeth, who
            lived in the side apartment; but
            on weekends the live-in staff
            has time off, replaced by Bev

who slept in the spare room
down in the basement)
I filled up my backpack with all the necessities—a
change of clothing and of course what I had left of the
Spice I kept stored away in my sock drawer.
I left my room key/house key in my bedroom since after all, I had no plan to return....

I slunk down the steps quietly, flicked my gaze around
the banister when I reached the bottom, and when I saw
that the coast was clear, eased the door open and slipped
on through swiftly and closed it softly behind me.
Then I was off—   first stop: Stewart's to buy me
some beer.

I bought, if I remember correctly, a twelve-pack of PBR
and a couple forties of either Steel Reserve or Old English and brought my purchases to the bridge and slunk
beneath it and sat on the ledge.
I cracked the first forty, brought the large bottle of Malt
Liquor to my lips, tipped it at a slight angle, and let the
bitter-sweet liquid stream out the nozzle and roll into
my mouth smoothly——the cold liquid, the strong, thick
taste, the instant rush as it hit my stomach, set my mind
ablaze and my head was buzzing, swimming in joy.... I
took another swig—euphoria.

I finished the bottle and pulled myself out from under
the bridge. With the booze tucked away in my backpack,
I followed the road as it unfolded downward, and it
brought me past Price Chopper and Walmart, and then
swung right, and I followed it past small establishments
interspersed with bars—and there were plenty of those.

My Cat Richie Dagger

The road split and came together, my head was buzzing with uncorrupted glee, my feet clumsily following the street as it curved and straightened, and took me upward and downward; and I was both lost and found all at once.

I found a nice spot on the curb in a residential area to sit down, looked both ways and all around me, and when I saw the coast was clear, started packing the Spice in my tiny metal one-hitter.

I finished packing it and propped it in my mouth, sparked the Bic lighter and brought it down on the Spice, and
as I inhaled, the smoke found its way easily through the pipe and into my mouth, and I sucked it down, and that previous swimming feeling I had felt started to get all loopy and everything suddenly changed colors—blue turned red, yellow turned pink, everything was backwards—and I stood up high as the moon and giddy as a loon, and walked away letting the fright of the night kick in————

although the plan to hitch a ride to Burlington must have slipped my mind by this point....

I followed the road back the way I'd come as it wound past more bars and more stores and I heard music coming from one of the bars and so I slipped through the door.

Open-Mike Night   apparently

Jeremy Void

I couldn't drink, I had no money, I spent the last of it on
the beer in my bag,   but I read at the open-mike

                    I read a poem called "Fuck You"
                        I read it and afterwards
                    I received good words, like:
"I wish I had the balls to read something like that."
"I wish there was a cop in here to hear that."

And then I left the bar, sat down and drank more, I
smoked more, I drank and smoked more, the smoke
streaming out of my mouth and swirling up to the sky—
it was amazing ...

and then my eyes opened and I was rising up and confused and my eyes were panning along and my vision
was seesawing, swaying, rolling, and it was dizzying and
I felt hazy and I pushed myself down from the ledge
and stumbled out from under the bridge, having a difficult time stabbing the sand with my feet to push myself
up the steep rise that curved around the bridge and
brought me to the street that rose over and dipped back
down, and I stood there swaying and staring out at the
black beyond
and then started back to the halfway house—my cellphone said it was 3 AM....

I had no key so I couldn't let myself in///
        Instead I banged and bashed the back door, I
racked and smacked the solid wood, and the door rattled
and ratcheted and jiggled and jammed inside the doorframe. I hit it again and again until I saw the lights in
the hallway in the basement flash on, one after another,

coming down the hall to meet me at the door, and there she was—
Bev was following the hallway, clearly just waking up, the fog in her eyes prominent in the dark of the night.

She opened the door and said, What's going on?

I spilled through the opening on uneasy feet, dropped my bag on the floor, and slurred, There's four beers in there.

What? she slurred right back.

I said there's four beers in there, as my body rocked to and fro.

I opened the bag and showed her, setting the beers on the floor beside it, and then picked up the bag and walked away and up the first set of stairs and through the hallway that led to the second set of stairs and then up those stairs too, and I pushed through my bedroom door and fell flat on my bed and passed out—just like that ...
       and in the morning I was so freaking hungover.

It was just another shitty night in my oh so shitty life.

** **

The next day, while I was out smoking a cigarette, feeling like a piece of crap—I mean what had gotten over me?—I saw a cat's head poking out of the bushes. For some reason I stuck out my hand and snapped my fingers together softly and the cat strolled right over.
This is my cat:
Richie Dagger,
named after the Germs' song
"Richie Dagger's Crime."

I always grew up with a dog, so I'm not used to having a cat, but this cat just grew on me. I never fed it while it hung out outside of Royce St. because I didn't want it to start relying on me until I could give it a proper home.
Every day it would sit outside the door meowing until I got home from work.

When I finally moved to my first apartment, I brought Richie along with me, only I didn't have a cage, so I just put him in the car beside me and the moment the doors opened, he bolted.
I had lost him, I thought.....
But he showed up back at Royce St. looking for me.
Smart cat...........................

So, ever since, I've taken care of this cat.......

Open-Mike Night at the 6B Lounge

On the train there was a group of jocks, a really cliché-looking bunch, going to the Red Sox game. Even though they all had thick Boston accents, they themselves weren't actually from Boston. I knew this because they weren't familiar with the subway system.

I thought I overheard one of them say they were getting off at Fenway—to see the Red Sox play at Fenway Park, no less. Which is totally absurd, if you ask me—you see, I have never been much of a baseball fan, let alone a sports fan, but I do know only out-of-towners get off at Fenway to see the Red Sox. Boston locals know the closest stop to Fenway Park is Kenmore, the stop right after Fenway.

When I lived in Boston I often attended shows at the Axis, which is now the House of Blues, located right behind Fenway Park. To get off for the Axis I'd always get off at Kenmore, because the Axis, or the House of Blues, is right around the corner.

So I said to the big militant guy sitting to my right, who in a way resembled Duke Nukem: Are you going to the Red Sox game?

Yeah, he said.

Getting off at Fenway?

Yeah.

Get off at Kenmore; it's closer. Fenway Park is right around the corner.

      There were seven of them, and when the train stopped at Fenway and the doors slid open, all but two got off, along with three quarters of the train, the passengers mobbing the doors and pouring out onto the street.
They're not from Boston, I said to the guy on my right, who had decided to take my advice, along with one other. Everyone from Boston, I continued, knows you get off at Kenmore.

And the two of them got off at Kenmore like I had sug-gested. I thought about their reactions when they ar-rived at Fenway Park well before their friends who had gotten off at Fenway because they didn't trust me much; they had said so rather openly and honestly before they left and went on their way.

I rode the rest of the way to Park Street in silence, got off, and walked up Beacon Street toward the 6B Lounge. Every Sunday night there's an open-mike there.

The first guy did a comedy routine that not many found funny. I found it to be rather lame myself.

Open-Mike Night at the 6B Lounge

I was up next, planning to read a very short story called "Nefarious Endeavor #2," featured in my very new book *Nefarious Endeavors.* I was leaning against a square column built before the stage ready to go up when the host approached me and said he thought it best to have a musical act go on next, as opposed to two spoken words in a row.
Whatever you think is best, I told him.

When the comedy routine was over, I decided to step out and have a smoke, but didn't feel like lugging my bag out there with me. So I left it in the booth where I was sitting, and asked an old guy nearby if he would watch it for me. A cute young girl, sitting at the table with him, said she'd watch it, and I said thanks, and stepped out.

When I finally went up to read, I blew them away, gaping jaws and wide eyes all around, people not knowing what to make of it, and it took a minute before they clapped. (I expected a somewhat stunned reaction.) But when they finally did, the host replaced me onstage and said, Now, *that's* how you deliver a story.

The girl who'd watched my bag when I stepped out for a smoke said, Good job, as I walked past.

I dropped off my bag, which I had kept beside me onstage, in the same booth, and again stepped out for a smoke.

When I came back in, that cute young girl had a guitar strapped to her. It looked as if she was getting ready to go up soon. I told her that when she was done she could feel free to peruse my book.

Turned out she was from Nashville, Tennessee, was on tour around America, and was the featured artist for the night. Although she played country, it sounded all right, and I left her a nice surprise with the host who said he'd deliver it to her when she was done, before I left—it was a signed copy of my new book *Nefarious Endeavors*, which I figured, if anything, she might show it to others she met on tour. (I thought, later on, I should have left my number in the book, because who knows? But then I decided it was probably better that I didn't since she wasn't planning on sticking around—and neither was I.)

For both instances I mentioned here—my telling the jocks, people I don't typically get along with, what stop to get off for Fenway Park; and my giving the girl from Nashville a free signed copy of *Nefarious Endeavors*—I didn't get to see their faces when they realized what I had done, for I left the bar before the girl was finished and I stayed on the train when the jocks got off. And it is killing me, because I want them to tell me they're grateful for what I'd done, to praise me, to raise my ego a bit, but that possibility has passed and doing a good deed for the sake of raising your ego takes the good right out of it.

But so does telling others about the act in the first place. The act was pure, I can assure you that; but the aftermath, like in any act of kindness, is getting to me.

A Forgotten Rebel—A Lost Soul

You see, I wasn't always treated like a ghost
   ——a distant memory....

Back when I was living in Boston I had many friends,
some closer than others. But they all knew who I was,
they respected me, they even put me on the pedestal I
like to think. Back then life was relentless, my existence
a complete mess, eroded by the frequent and excessive
consumption of drugs and alcohol.
I was out to lunch, as this one guy, Joe, used to say every
time I saw him. One night I stabbed that dirty skinhead
in the arm cuz he reached out and tried to snatch one of
my beers after I already told him no

                     but, feeling slightly bad about
                     what I had done—for this was a
                     friend of mine—I had offered
                     him my T-shirt to clean up the
                     blood. As all this was going
                     down, a dirty, roughneck squat-
                     ter who had arrived via bicycle
                     said in a deep, scratchy voice,
                     calm and calculating, he said,
                     I'll fucking shoot you in the

face if you pull that shit
again....
(Okay, maybe I adlibbed there, as his threat was a bit less
abrasive-sounding, a bit less aggressive, more like: *I've
got a gun and you keep fucking around like that, drawing un-
wanted attention to our spot, I'm not afraid to use it.*)

So, how did the story end? you
might be asking:

Chuck and I ripped the fucker off, we stole his entire
frame pack full of all his shit that he carried around
with him—teach him to think twice about threating *me*
with a fucking gun, *please!*
—in which I found nothing of value, only a sleeping bag,
a book of phone numbers, possibly work contacts, and a
pair of damp, smelling socks balled up and stuffed in the
bottom, so the whole thing was kind of a waste;
but hey, at least we got the last laugh
out of all this————and we did
laugh!
............*A LOT*.......

WE WERE ALWAYS fucking LAUGHING, everything was a
joke to me and the people I chilled with——people knew
me as Jeremy St. Chaos back then, master of destruction,
seeker of adventure....
I got talking to these two
kids outside of a show at
Regeneration Records,
back when they used to
house shows there, that
is—

I believe we were standing in line at the time
                     —and after talking for a
                     while about this and that,
                     getting to know one an-
                     other—
which I always found is the case, Punk to Punk
                     —shooting the shit, they
                     gave me their names and
                     I gave them mine:

                     Jeremy St. Chaos.

                     At the single utterance
                     of that name both their
                     jaws dropped and their
                     eyes widened, two sus-
                     pended jaws, and four
                     wide-open eyes staring
                     at me in wonder and ex-
                     citement.
                           Y-y-y-you're Jer-
                     emy St. Chaos, said the
                     first one to break the si-
                     lence—
I don't think he actually stuttered, but I'm sure you get
the point
                     —and I nodded curiously,
                     wondering what's with
                     the shared feeling of
                     shock & awe between
                     these two Punk rockers.

Jeremy Void

Then the other one said:
You hang out with
Shawnasey, right?

Again I nodded, with a
devilish smirk obscuring
my face, and an overall
feeling of excitement
that these two knuckle-
brains have heard of me
before this night—
they told me I was, like, a legend, and they elaborated by
telling me some of my own claims to fame—most of
which were exaggerations, and the rest were fabrica-
tions, but still

—and then the line
started to move and its
cruising speed as it
curved through the door
pulled me along easily,
and before long I was in
the venue, only to get
thrown back out again
once the band played
Black Flag's "Depression."

See, this is exactly what I'm talking about. People knew
who I was, they admired me, they adored me, I was infa-
mous to the mass public and famous to a small group of
fuckups ... but that's all I need in the end:
the adoration of some lost fuckups who waste their time
skateboarding, no less, and going to Punk rock shows, and

100

they're mean and crude, and they're my kind of people
too///

Guess that could still be true in a smaller sense, that I'm
adored by lost souls spending all their time trying to
figure out what for, analyzing the whys and wherefors,
searching for meaning on a planet the size of a town, on
an island surrounded by fishermen who can't see them
at all.

But today/
>>>>>>>>>>>>>>>>>>>and yesterday too
and most likely tomorrow
I am a nobody, even more lost than my lost would-be
fans///

I'm a ghost, a distant memory—forgotten and despised,
so lost and sad and full of spite—and I will break out in
hives if you don't start acknowledging me soon. I will
get an ulcer. I will claw out my own fucking eyes

and the last thing I would see on this Godforsaken planet
is my own reflection staring back at me, leering like a
crazed loonytune....

But hey, don't you laugh at me
because it isn't funny....
not in the least bit///

Hahahah
>>>okay, maybe just a little

Everyone Died

earlier today someone asked me about what had drawn me to the life i'd chosen. i'll start with that.

when i was younger i was with a girl in my old bedroom, and she went rummaging through my closet. she came out with a thick black notebook that had letters taped to the front, spelling "my portfolio." she opened it to take a look inside. it was the portfolio i put together throughout my time in elementary school.

the first day of second grade: *How Was Your Summer?*

Sucked, i had written.

Why?

Everyone Died.

on the following page was a crass rendering of my entire family, all with x's etching out their eyes.

that was me as a kid.

something about death attracted me. maybe it was my curiosity. which was why d.a.r.e. didn't work for me. they said Drugs were bad. Period. but why would some-body do them, then? what's the catch? so i had to find out.

Drugs made me feel ... *awesome.*

they didn't hook me with their addictive tentacles, like d.a.r.e. had predicted. well, not right away, anyway.

when asked in high school what i wanted to be when i grew up, i said, rather curtly, *A Mobster.*

A Serial Killer.

A Drug Dealer.

a junky?

i seeked Danger, and i found Danger. it came at me swinging and knocked me flat on my back. Danger was dangerous, i found out; it would bite off my arm.

i learned the hardest lesson of all: life is unforgiving. when provoked, it will come out kicking. and trust me, i've taken a boot to my ribs many a time.

> so you're asking me Why?
> Why would i seek out that life?

it's simple, really. what else was there to do? growing up in the city can be quite boring at times. sure, there was an endless amount of excitement, but nothing exciting enough to draw me in.

well, except for that.
      except for this.
            some people get their kicks from Eating.
            some people get their kicks from Sex.
            some people Gamble away their lives.
            for what?
well, we've all got our vices.
and the one i chose (choose) will ... *[drumroll]* ... make you high!
      but what can you expect?
      from a drug addict such as me
      a nobody and a fiend
      a liar and a thief....

you see, i lived the life, i did the time,   (... the lie),
but
that doesn't mean i understand it.

  i'm an Addict, and that's all you need to know about it.
  so stop pestering me with all your nosey questions!

A Stranger in a World Filled with Strange People

This morning I awoke in an all-white room. It wasn't the room where I normally sleep. It was smaller, devoid of artwork and posters I've previously hung up on the walls. Directly in front of me the wall angled to form a sharp triangle with the wall to my left. It scared the crap out of me. The lights were off, and for a moment I thought I was in the hospital again.

I squirmed around, taking in the shape and the blank décor of the room. I squirmed some more, eyes wide with fright.

I searched frantically for the light, a light, any light, just something to shine light on my situation— literally, *and* figuratively.

My eyes darted from one blank, white wall to the next. In the dark.
Then it hit me....
There was a lamp on my right side, right beside the bed I had slept on. I reached out and turned the nob and light instantly flooded the room.

I was in my grandmother's old house, which my parents had just recently inherited, renovated, and made their own. They had deemed my grandmother's

old office as my bedroom when I come up here to stay
with them,

> because the other
> rooms in the
> house are bigger
> and thus better
> suited for married
> couples, like my
> brother and his
> wife, and my sis-
> ter and her hus-
> band.

So I'm the lucky one who gets stuck with the smaller
room that only fits one person....

> Yay me!

Not that I really want to get involved with anyone in
particular, or at all, for that matter, but it would be nice
to have someone who I can share my hell with—by "my
hell," I mean my world.

I guess I'm a terminal loner. I've always been out-
cast from everything I stuck my feet into. Always. I'm
weird——so what? There are plenty of weird people in
the world—just not to the same degree as me, I suppose.
I'm a stranger in a world filled with strange people.

I've only got me. No wonder I'm such a narcissist.
It became a defense mechanism growing up. If no one
was going to think about me, then I'll just think about
myself.

... plain and simple ...

In Burlington Today

> In Burlington today I got a new book and on the drive
> home read six or seven chapters straight while Nirvana
> (gross!) played on the stereo, with the only break to type
> this post and let everyone know.
>
> Andrew Smith is a sick fucking author. I'm within the
> last 50 pages of his book *The Passenger* and today I
> picked up his book *Grass Hopper Jungle* at Phoenix
> Books in Burlington, VT, this afternoon.
>
> — Jeremy Void, via Facebook

This coffee sucks, and I'd never seen a coffee so small.
Biggest coffee shop I'd ever been inside of, smallest coffee I'd ever laid my eyes upon. Guess it's compensation,
in a weird sense of the word. And it cost a buck seventy-
five. I got a coffee four times the size for equal the
price, maybe a nickel more, at the gas station on my way
here>>>>>>>>>>>>>>>>>>

Here!   *Where is here????*

                                   Burlington, VT
                                   I am in Burlington.
Rode up with a cast of characters I'm not particularly
fond of, but hey they kept quiet for most the ride, and
the drive itself wasn't too bad; got some reading done.

Sitting at home obsessing
about this and that—book
stuff——hasn't helped
the process much: my
focus and the like....

But the doofuses are gone now,
and now I am here alone,
in the biggest coffee shop I'd ever been inside of, gingerly sipping the smallest coffee I'd ever held in my
hand, around a nasty sort of grimace that I can't control
right now, the coffee tastes so bad.

But anyway, I'm glad to be out of Rutland and in Burlington today,,,,,,, even if for only one and a half hours—
hahahah, seriously!—having endured a two-hour ride
with a group of cretins that deserve a cringe rather
than a proper hello when I bump into them on the
street.

But on the drive they kept quiet
and for that
I am quite grateful/

So   first stop Phoenix Books, where I picked up
another book by Andrew Smith (I'm currently within the
final fifty pages of his book *The Passenger*, the sequel to
The Marbury Lens) for a rather decent price—ten dollars
and change———and they said they'd carry my books on
consignment, just bring em in—yay me!——and they'll
only take 60% of the cut—*only????*
                    Which kinda sucks!   But hey
it's better than the 80% the used bookstore in Rutland
was asking for, or the fact that the Phoenix Books that

just recently opened in Rutland won't sell them at all ("because it's a family store," said the old hag who works there—*a family store? please!).*

So here I am, in Burlington, VT, at the biggest coffee shop I'd ever been inside of, gingerly sipping the smallest coffee I'd ever laid eyes upon, with a measly cringe—*yuck!!!!*

Tonight Ryan and I are going to record some of Spark Plugs tracks over at his place and then perform them for the rather dull crowd that comes to Pub 42's open-mikes on Sunday nights.   (They're dull because everybody who performs there plays only covers, I haven't seen a single one of them do anything close to original—except me——and because nobody there appreciates good poetry like I do, or even good art to start with....

FUCKERS!

But tonight, with our new, raw sound, our punishing brand of noise, wrapped with my own delightfully mean and wonderfully rhythmic— what with my remarkable choice of words—poetry that comes at you like a soaring, corkscrewing jackknife that flies overhead and curves around like a swooping jet-plane and hits you in the back with a sharp, devastating suckerpunch that knocks you flat on your knees/

Like a streetfighting junky
like an asskicking crackhead
like a speedfreak with the arms
of a ninja robot

>>>>>>>>>> just   like   that

It's no joke——   Straight up noise, fierce,
ferocious, and volatile, an electronic roar, a supersonic
dogbite, weaved with visceral wordplay that'll rip your
spleen out through your asshole and hang it up on a
clothesline so that the bloody member will dry squeak-
ily clean—*that's* the power behind our original sound—***a***
stungun in your fuckin face!———no joke!!!

But anyway, I gotta
go now—it's two-
o'clock and my
ride should
be leaving soon///

An Unsent Letter to My Hero

"I'd rather write a poem than be a person any day."
— Richard Hell

To Richard Meyers
a.k.a. Richard Hell

I'm not your biggest fan. I don't want to start this letter off by saying that, cuz I'm sure tons of people have made that claim. I don't want you to think I'm just another cliché. Which I am; we all are. But that's aside the point.

I am a big fan. Why? Because I've never related to anybody's writing like I have to yours. I am a recovering crack head, and your writing has helped me recover, majorly.

Where do I start? How about this:

{insert "a poem for richard hell" in *An Art Form: The Crass Poetry Collection*}

** ⧗ **

As the poem says, I first found your album *Blank Genera-tion* a couple days before I turned 19 and I bought it for myself as a birthday present. Right away I fell in love with your music, your style, your everything.

Shortly after that I bought your book *Hot and Cold,* and that was the first book I'd ever owned. There's video footage of me and a couple friends blowing lines of coke off the surface of it.

When I was 22 and in treatment for drugs and alcohol and numerous other problems I had to deal with, being that I was bored out of my skull, I read your novel *Go Now.* That was the first novel I ever read, and it got me addicted to reading. In *Go Now,* when the main character does heroin, it was like I was doing heroin. When he has sex, it was like I was having sex. It was so visceral and I loved it. (I try to write that way myself, and I like to think I succeed, and people certainly have said so.) I've shared *Go Now* with so many of my friends, most of whom are in recovery themselves, and they all say it's too much. But for me, it hit the spot.

Aside from that, your writing has helped me so much through the beginning of my recovery.

Plus, I got started writing when I read your quote from *Hot and Cold:* "If you bring yourself to write for long enough you'll eventually say something interesting." Af-ter reading that, on a whim, I decided to start journaling. That was about 5 years ago, and since then I have written and published 7 books. Although I always wrote, as I sang for a Punk band called Lethal Erection for 5 years and I wrote all the lyrics, I never got into seriously writing for the sake of writing until I read that quote.

Currently I am a few months past 1 year sober, after 4 years of not being able to put together a mere 90 days. I assume you frequent AA/NA yourself because in your notebook in *Hot and Cold*, you say things that sound like AA/NA references, but then, I could be wrong about all that. You might have just been to a few AA/NA meetings and picked up some of the jargon, but never really stuck with it. But if you do, I thought that knowing I'm a member and I've struggled desperately in the past years trying to get sober might count for something, and knowing that your writing and your music has helped me on my way might count for even more.

I've included here two of my books: *Just a Kid* and *Nefarious Endeavors.* I would love nothing more than for you to tell me what you think. As I said, you have been my biggest inspiration, and maybe it would be worth it for you to see what that means. It would be cool if I could get your permission to insert your review on one of my books, or even on my website. But if you'd rather I not, I'll respect your wishes, because it would be plenty cool if you wrote back and told me what you thought in the first place.

Thank you so so much,
— Jeremy Void

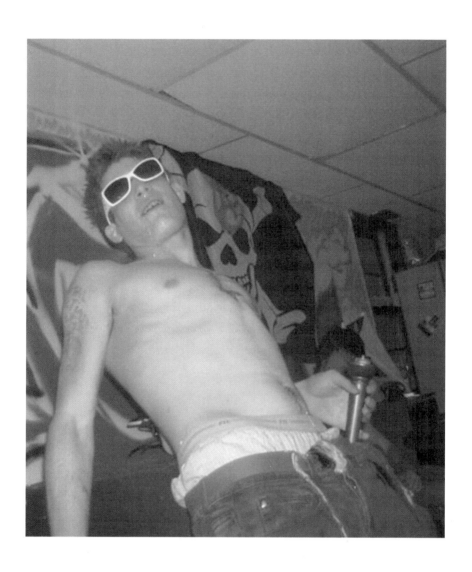

On Poetry

"I started writing because it was so easy. I saw all this writing being praised and I knew I could do better with a splitting headache on the subway at rush hour. Most poets are bullshitters—they have so many vested interests, from keeping their associate professorship to keeping their self-respect, whereas I hardly have any interests at all."

— Theresa Stern

At the NA meeting today I saw my old sponsor. My current sponsor, who I've been working with for close to three years now, is an avid AA-goer, and prefers the old-school Twelve Steps of AA. I'm apt to agree with him on that, because I tried the NA Step Guide with my old sponsor, and it just didn't work for me. It's basically a workbook filled with questions, each question pertaining to a particular Step. While working the Steps that way I was always told there are no wrong answers. I just had to answer each and every question honestly—or as honest as possible at the time, which wasn't very honest at all—and then I moved on to the next Step. See, that doesn't exactly sit right with me—doesn't really make much sense.

If a Step One question asked me if I was powerless over drugs, and I responded with No, should I still go on to the next Step? Because if I don't feel that I am powerless, I haven't done the Step.
But then, I didn't fully feel like I was powerless over drugs and alcohol until I got to Step Four. Everything comes in time, I guess.

But anyway:
So I ran into this old sponsor of mine. About three years ago—shortly after I had fired him as my sponsor and immediately found a new one—I ran into him at a meeting at which he said in a share that he started writing a book of poetry. This was three years ago, remember. About a year and a half ago, shortly after I came out with *Derelict America*, I saw him at a meeting and told him about my book. I could see it in his face that he was right away hit with spite, and it hit him hard.
After a thought or two rolled through his head, and he had some time to calm himself down, he asked if it was a book of poetry.
No, short stories, I said.
I hadn't started writing prose until after I'd fired him as a sponsor, so this took him by surprise.
I even showed him a bit from "Freedom in America," which is less of a story and more of a personal essay, and he chuckled bitterly, uttering something like, That's just poetry.
It definitely didn't sit well with him that he had been working on a book of poetry for longer than I had been writing *Derelict America*, I could tell, and he continued to

make snide remarks regarding my book for the rest of the night—a group of us from NA that night went to Burger King after the meeting, him and myself included.

But anyway, poetry is a crapshoot. "Most poets are bullshitters" said Theresa Stern, one of my favorite poets—I wanted to include the rest of that quote here but I couldn't find the book that I had found it in, *Hot and Cold* by Richard Hell, on my shelves. But oh well, the gist of what she said is:
She said she could do better with a splitting headache on the subway during rush hour. She named her own favorite poet, said he's the smartest guy she'd ever met, and claimed his poetry doesn't make any sense.
Interpret that however you wish, for I have my own interpretations and don't wish to muddy yours.

But I'll get back to that.

So, this old sponsor of mine, I saw him today, and like always he greeted me with a hug, asked me how I was doing, and I told him shamelessly that my second book will be out soon. As I said that he turned his back on me and immediately went to greet someone else who was just walking in. I could tell this bothered him, or maybe I was reading his body language incorrectly, as I often do. Either way, I wrote two books before he wrote one.

This feels good, I can't deny it. And I'll tell you why: It shows that I'm better at something than someone else, and I'll be the first to admit that that kind of thinking is wrong, but for now it's the only kind of thinking that I've got, and while it's mine I might as well own it   right?

Life's too short to live in shame, anyway.

                        So, poetry, why is it a crapshoot? (I'm not entirely sure I'm even using the word "crapshoot" correctly though.)

Because it's easy. At least for me it is. Poems don't need to make sense, they're mostly just a series of words, a series of sentences, a series of stanzas, randomly ordered in a verbal array of nonsense. I mean, some poems have meaning, and in some poems, even, the poet intended for there to be meaning. But great poetry doesn't have to have any meaning at all, that's what makes them great, I suppose. A well-written poem has depth, whether or not the poet intended it. So anyone can write a poem, and there are so many different kinds that anyone can find one suitable for their own style of writing. They can be abstract, surreal, or based in reality; they can be meaningful, meaningless, or just plain retarded; they can rhyme, but they don't have to rhyme.

That said, since you can easily cater your poem to your own particular style of writing, deeming a poem as good or bad is utterly impossible. That's why it's a crapshoot.

On Poetry

Although for the record, I have nothing against poetry; I think it's a great way to express oneself, because it's so easy anyone can do it.

Life Is Good   I Think

Last night I sent out for an ISBN number for this new
      book called *The Lost Letters/*
I redid the launch page at www.chaoswriting.net/
I redid the homepage on my site too/
                      I finished proofreading
                      The Lost Letters/
                      and put it all together in
                      its finality/

I finished typing up some more of my blogs for my next
      book, which might be called *Apathetic, Hopeless, and*
      in Love—it's going to be a collection of random
      rants and ramblings, very experimental and
      chaotic/
I posted a bunch of poems and visual poems on
      deviantART/
                  —————so I'd say I got a lot done/

Of course
I didn't get any sleep last night, which is a given if I put
in that many hours))))
                        Life is good,
                        I think....

My Writing Group—no more!

At my creative writing group Friday I got cut off when I was just about done with the poem I was reading because nobody wanted to hear about me hocking loogies on someone, said Sh----, the facilitator of the group.

Which is such bullshit because weeks earlier she said we can read whatever we want without having to worry about offending anyone.

This really pissed me off because
1. the poem, like just about all my pieces, was very personal to me;
2. I was just about at the end anyway;
3. and she was searching for a reason to cut me off from the getgo.

Before I read, I said "You guys are going to love this piece" in a sarcastic tone, and so before I started reading she stopped me and said that means they probably won't love it.

I actually thought they would, in fact, love it. The reason I said that before I read wasn't because of the

part about hocking loogies, it was because of the use of the word geezer,
and the group is mostly made up of
senior citizens.

But turns out, she was put off by the part about hocking
loogies.

Which I also think is a cop-out to the real issue.

I once read a piece about
lighting two Punk rock-
ers (*guys,* no less) on fire
and the piece was loaded
with vulgarities and was
even racially charged. I
think *that* piece, by far,
was the most violent and
offensive piece I've written.

But, apparently not:
she let me read it all the
way through without
interrupting me or even
commenting afterwards
that she was offended.
Months later I read an-
other piece that was no-
where near as offensive
as the former piece but
she commented after-
wards about the
mentioning of beating up
a pregnant chick. She
was absolutely appalled
by it.

My Writing Group—no more!

That said<<<   I think the real issue was the line "And we stand / around & spit the balls of phlegm on the fallen / man or woman—either one works—who takes it like...." cuz it was right at that point when she cut me off.
God forbid I spit loogies on <u>women</u>, but it's okay to spit them on men, right?
The reason I wrote "man or woman" was to show equality; not to single any sex out.

Earlier in the group we were talking about a hobby store in Rutland, and one woman said the management there is sexist and she therefore chooses not to shop there.
Sh----, on the other hand, replied that yes, they are in fact sexist—thus *no one* should shop there. How close-minded is that?

The whole world should be punished because one group of people disapproves of someone else's morals. For all I care, you can think whatever the fuck you want because nobody—and I mean *nobody* in this entire fucking world—is right about anything. How could they be?
(((We all think we are, we all think we have the answers, but nobody knows anything about anything)))))))))

This is why I do not like hippies. Or feminists. I am not sexist, nor am I racist, but I reserve the right to express myself however I choose, and if that means write something that could be construed as sexist, you'll be damn sure I will.

Art has no bounds/
Anything goes/

       the way I see it.......................................

All the time I hear things in my writing group that I
disagree with myself, but do I say their pieces are bad or
even cut them off before they are finished?
NO, I FUCKING DON'T!
because it's none of my business what they write..

So I walked out of the group on Friday. I said I'd come
back in two weeks, since I'll be out of town next weekend—although come to think of it, I don't actually leave
until well after the writing group ends on Friday—but
after thinking about it, and I did think about it a lot, I've
decided that I'd rather not attend anymore.
I can't relate to most of them there, and I don't even see
why I go in the first place...

Meeting a New/Old Friend

I had a strange night last night:

It started at an appointment I had with a therapist and a doctor. I'm planning to move back to Boston soon, and two things I need in place before I move are a therapist and a doctor.

The therapist, after I showed him my books, told me about a place in Arlington called Right Turn, which is an art/recovery center for alcoholics and drug addicts. They hold an AA meeting every night, plus other events more oriented toward art. So I decided to check it out.

I got to Arlington at around six-o'clock, found a Starbucks, got a coffee, and sat down. The AA meeting itself started at seven, but I left the Starbucks and headed to Right Turn at six-thirty because, one, I

wanted to explore the place before the meeting started and,
two, it's always better to arrive
at a meeting somewhat early.

The place was really nice.
On the walls hung various
paintings and musical records.
I thought it all rather fascinat-
ing.

So, the meeting unexpect-
edly ran until eight-thirty. At
this particular meeting I wasn't
allowed to speak because the
group conscious had decided
that only those who've completed the Twelve Steps could
speak. There's a similar meeting in Rutland, which even
though I only attended it once I
rather enjoyed.

I liked it *because* I couldn't
speak, and *because* others who
haven't completed the Steps
couldn't speak, either; it keeps
the poisonous talk to a mini-
mum.

After the meeting, since I
wasn't sure what time the bus-
ses ran till, I hitched a ride to
Harvard Square from a guy
who introduced himself to me
right at the start of the meeting. In the car I asked him if

he would sponsor me when I
moved to Boston, because my
sponsor in Rutland was the
first person in AA to talk to me
there, so I figured since this
guy was the first to talk to me
here, I'd give him a shot. But,
unfortunately, he already had
four sponsees, and he said that
was his limit.

But still, when he pulled to a
stop right in front of the Coop
in Harvard Square, he gave me
his card because, he said, who
knows how many sponsees he
will have when I finally move
to Boston?

I thanked him, stepped out of the car, and
shut the door.
Immediately two drunken teens approached me saying
they had lost their shoes. I laughed at that and walked
away. Lit a cigarette and crossed the street to the train
station.

On the other side of the street I
turned around because I really
had to pee and went back to the
Coop to use their bathroom.
The Coop is a huge bookstore,
and on my way out I bought
two books, then left and lit another cigarette and crossed the
street and took a seat at the top

of the escalator to finish my
smoke.
Then around the corner emerged a fairly short girl who
stopped before me in utter shock——
That was when things got strange.

Jeremy! she said.
Yeah. Who are you? I replied.
I can't believe it's you.
Seriously, who are you? She looked fa-
miliar, but I still couldn't place her.
She told me her name—it was Molly.
Now, I was shocked. *From Facebook?*
Yeah, she said.

About four weeks ago someone named Molly added me
as a friend on Facebook. About two weeks ago she messaged me and asked if I remembered her. I didn't. She
said we used to go to shows together. I went on her page
and scanned through her photos and told her she looked
familiar but I still couldn't place her. Then we chatted at
length, before she said she had work in the morning and
had better go.
So seeing her there last night was so
strange—kind of like serendipitous. Like it was meant to
happen. Like fate.

She eventually told me her real
name was Vanessa—or, as people used to call her, Nessa. That
was when it hit me. Dan Baker
and I went and visited her in
Amherst, MA, where she used to

live when I was, like, seventeen
or sixteen. But I don't remember ever seeing her at shows,
though. In fact that time at
Amherst was the only time I
remember ever seeing her. As
the years passed, I always won-
dered what happened to that
girl I met at Amherst all those
years ago. Because I don't
remember ever seeing her
again. Maybe the only reason I
remember her at Amherst was
because I was somewhat sober
during our visit—well, except
for those six shots of espresso
Dan Baker's aunt had bought
me at the coffee shop.

In the Pit she showed me her art, I showed her my new
book, we talked for a while, catching up, and then we
rode the train together.
On the train I asked her if she'd draw me a picture of a
Punk rock chick playing with herself so that I could
hang it on my wall and she could sign her name on it,
along with her website, or whatever she calls that site
that showcases her art. She said she would, and I really
hope she follows through because that would be so sick.
Then I got off at Park Street,
awkwardly said bye (for I suck at saying bye), and
headed home.

Boston?

I want to go to Boston because ...

           I want to go to Boston because I think it will help me get to where I want to go. Which is, I don't know. I'm not sure. I want to be a successful writer but I don't think that's possible so it seems easier to not even try. People say I'm a great writer, even though I know they're mostly lying or coddling me or maybe even trying to deceive me for their own sick enjoyments— there's numerous reasons why they might be telling me I'm great.

Or maybe I *am* great.

This query upsets me. The thinking of it doesn't upset me; what upsets me is that I will never know because I can either put my trust in people or not. Either way, the answer is still the same, which is I will never know.

But on to other subjects—such as Boston.

I want to go, but I don't want to go, but I want to go, but I don't want to go, but I want to go, but I don't want to go, and this kind of ambivalence upsets me so I try not to even bother coming up with a decision.

It's easier not to think about it. Out of sight, out of mind, as they say. But the future is coming too, as they say. But they also say the future is unwritten. Or at least that's what Joe Strummer said. For all I know staying in Rutland might be the most beneficial of the two decisions. Or if I went to Burlington, I might by chance meet Stephen King and he might by chance read one of my books—or all of them. I could go to California and get hit by a bus. I could go to New York and win the lottery. I could get on TV if I go to Texas.

There are cornfields in Kanas.

Right now I'm in Rutland and I don't fucking mind it. There are people I hate and there are people I like. There are people I hate in Boston too, so what's the difference? I know I'm sucking ⌊myself⌋ dry every fucking day from being here and I don't want to do that. But I can't make it up no matter what I do. Unless I go to Washington and win the lottery. Or was that Utah?

I could steal a boat and ride it to the Bermuda Triangle and never come back. Surely I could do that. I once stole a paddleboat and rode it to an island inhabited by wild geese—true story. And I stood there in the cold, by myself, having to pee, so I pulled down my pants and pissed where I was because if I moved the wild geese would peck off my pecker—I don't want to go there again. Although I wouldn't mind going to an island all by myself and calling it home—and when I say all by myself, I mean the island has yet to be discovered and I could name it whatever I pleased.

But what do I think about Boston?

I don't.

Shitless in Sobriety

Why am I such a pussy?

Like, just now, I stood outside of this house in Stowe, it's 2:05 AM, and I lit my cigarette and sucked in the smoke, when I heard the clickety-clack of tree branches snapping, the rustle of leaves swaying and scattering and brushing, and the rickety-rack of rocks and stones skittering to a stop on the ground; I see lights in the distance, hear the steady breathing of something or another which comes across as ominous in the dead of the night, out here in the middle of the countryside, and what do I do?—I chuck the cigarette butt, yank the door open, and slam through the doorway, my body shaking, my breath coming out harsh and uneven, my legs wobbly, my whole being explosive and frightened, and now I'm here writing about it—thinking it's worthy enough to be featured in one of my books== the narcissism of it all.

Like, spiders freak me out; I can't go near just one, small—and I mean nearly microscopic in size—or large, nor do I do spider webs, active or abandoned. Cob webs, white and soggy, hanging from the pines of a bush, just sitting there unattended and old and decaying, waiting for someone to take a vacuum to it and suck it into the void—no, they freak the shit out of me too....

Why am I such a pussy?
I remember years ago, early in sobriety, I was afraid of so much more, like when I attended shows I developed a fear of my own friends, fellow Punk rockers who I always say are the kindest, most genuine people I've ever met—well, for the most part—although problems obviously occur as is the case with any group of social misfits, I mean there's a reason they deviate from the herd.... They're accepting and easy-going; sure they're rough around the edges, but like I said, that's a given when you're dealing with kids in exile, kids estrange from the "normal" swing of things....
Although there is, as I'm encountering now, a group of Punk rockers called Crusty Punks, and these are people worth fearing, what with their liberal agendas and politically correct course of action. There weren't as many of them in Boston, there were some but I had deemed them Hippies with Mohawks, or Peace Punks, as others might call them. They were rare and mostly hated, they hung out with their own and even had their own brand of Punk rock so that they wouldn't mingle with us true believer, us who wanted a free world....

But here in Vermont, they're a domineering species/

But anyway, I digressed.
I mean, my own freaking friends! Afraid of what they might do if they caught me in a dark alley, in a dank and

dirty basement located beneath some rough dive bar of
some sort. Afraid????
> I partied with these kids
> We smoked and did lines together
> We drank and did it up
> We lit up the night, set it bright on fire
> We ran amok in Rutland, VT
> > scaring the oh so "friendly"
> bystanders

> We had fun
> > fun
> > > FUN
> > > > and now I'm the scared one!!!

Why am I so damn frightened of everything?
> and everyone?

Must be why I drank in the first place, drank and got
high off all sorts of different things—so I didn't have to
deal with my nagging anxieties, it was a form of self-
medicating—a form of self-degradation—it was just
something I did to get by ...

and now, without it, I'm a total fucking pussy!

I'm scared and livid of just about everything that comes
my way .... why? I used to be so tough, so hardcore, a British bulldog I was, a guy who never turned
down a fight—even though I lost most often, guess I
never learned how to fight, you would have thought I
would have picked up something or another from all the
scruffs I had entered, but no, nothing—a guy who was
mean and disagreeable, a Jewish kid who sported a

Jeremy Void

Swastika on his shirt because he didn't give a fuck all
about what others thought, about their prejudgments
and assessments, and their petty bullshit that comes
from ignorance and blissful living, sleeping away one's
life—I didn't care about you or what you thought of me
                                        and yet, a few days ago I
walked around Rutland, VT, in my old DESTROY T-shirt,
which even though it has the Swastika right on the front
in plain sight is anti-fascist, anti-religion, and anti–
government, and I was scared out of my diseased mind
of what others thought, of what if someone tries to fight
me, cuz I wasn't prepared at all; there's a black dude
coming my way, I better act quick and cover up the
Swastika somehow—
                        I was constantly grabbing my flannel shirt
and pulling it in front so that it hopefully covered it up,
but
                                        it didn't
                                        I know,
it never did, it was futile, and I failed like everything
else in life/

So I'm scared. A year ago or maybe more the doctor took
me off of Klonopin and that was when the anxiety hit
me full-force, anxiety with which I was mostly unfamil-
iar, it was always there, but just foreign, trilling about in
the back of my mind, my nerves near dead as the K-pin
took ahold of my blood and numbed me drastically———
                        I miss those days....

But don't you see

Shitless in Sobriety

(you're too numb to see anything)
don't you know, this Jeremy Void, formerly known as
the fearless Jeremy St. Chaos, master of destruction,
seeker of adventure, is scared)))))

The world is a scary place when you don't got drugs to
relax your fears, to lessen your crazed anxieties—I
know all about it, trust me I do....

144

What the Hell Is Wrong with Me?

I'm going to Stowe this afternoon. A few months ago, amid a serious depression, I went up to Stowe for the sake of a change of scenery. Cuz maybe that would shake me loose from my depression. Also, since my depressions usually contain a degree of self-loathing and my self-loathings usually consist of me thinking I'm a terrible writer because that's just about all I've got going for me right now, I was feeling in a giving mood and in Stowe I gave away a few free copies of my books. I have a hard time asking people to buy my books—especially people I don't know—without some degree of opening, some lead-in that would present myself as a published author with books for sale (like what open-mikes offer me); but I find it a lot easier to give out my books for free——since all I have to do for that is approach a random person and say, "Do you want a free book," and nobody ever turns down a free anything; but to say do you want to buy a book from me, who would be stupid enough to take up that offer, anyway?

Not me!

So I went to the coffee shop and offered to give the kids working there a free book, and the young guy said I should talk to the blond-haired girl I saw there earlier that day because she's into dark writing like this and in fact, surprisingly enough, she does her own writing of a darker nature. It was surprising because she looked like a total ditz from first glance—but then, you can never really know.

(I remember when she was in at the coffee shop working earlier in the day I overheard her say to one of the other girls there that she was single—well, it was more in the context of, "Why are you single?" asked the other girl there. And this caught my attention for some reason. I'm not sure why I remember this specific detail of their conversation and nothing else; but I did.)))

So that night, at the house in Stowe, I wrote her a poem that I would share to her on the following day, and that's what I did.

I approached her the next day and asked if she likes poetry, and she said yes—and there was a nervous, frightened undertone in her voice, she seemed so damn jumpy when I first approached her there, like what is this fucking freak doing talking to *me* of all people? but even so she didn't shoo me away like I had expected her to do (yeah, I know, I'm a bit paranoid too), and at first her voice was layered with a trembling ambience that I interpreted as fear—but it surely settled the more we talked.

And then I told her I wrote a poem last night that I was hoping to read to her today, and she said shoot, and I read it, and it was definitely of the serenade variety, which is why I called it "The Serenade" and put it right in the beginning of *The Lost Letters,* but unfortunately for the both of us, when I finished reading it to her, I said I didn't write it for her. It was just a general poem that definitely did seem like a pick-up kind of poem that I wrote for no one in particular, being the nervous little prick I am, always so afraid of rejection (*what the hell is wrong with me????*); and then we talked some more and she said she was a fan of Kerouac and I gave her a copy of *Just a Kid.*

That said, I've been to that coffee shop many times since, and I've seen her there each time, and each time I think about asking her out—and each time she acts awkward and afraid which only feeds me with more doubt—and each time I get too nervous, reading her strangeness around me as a preemptive rejection———like, I made an ass of myself a few months ago and now all our interactions from here on out will always be awkward.
(*what the hell is wrong with me????*)

So, I'm going up to Stowe this afternoon and I'm thinking maybe this time will be different, maybe this time I'll work up the nerve to finally talk to her again; but then I remember that I say that every time I'm about to go to Stowe and every time it's all the same.
For all I know, her acting nervous and jittery may very well be a character trait of hers, although she didn't seem that way until after I first approached her all that time ago—but then, I might not have noticed it until afterwards because I'm more conscientious about it now.
Or maybe—and I could only hope—she wants to go out with me too and she reads my own

strangeness as a preemptive rejection. Or as noncha-
lance—or indifference—which is the appearance I tend
to generate when I'm nervous, I think.

Or maybe not.
I don't know.
I never do know.
All I know is that whatever I choose to do will work out
the way it's going to work out
and I should just have faith in the grand scheme of
things because fear only stops you from experiencing
more than you could ever imagine is possible.

I keep telling myself this, and yet I never do work up
the courage to act.... 		(*what the hell is wrong with me????*)

A Group of Drunks

I'm feeling really anxious right now, bored too, and I don't know why. I looked at the time, thinking this meeting must be over soon, but it's only twelve-thirty—I got a half an hour left.

I brought up the topic at this meeting. My younger sister got married about a month ago, and my older brother is getting married in a week. But what about me???? I'm alone==   hopelessly, utterly alone, with nobody and no hope to speak of. But it isn't all about that, though. I just feel like I got a shit deal in life. That's what it's about.

I've heard a lot of good stuff here. Make a gratitude list every day, one guy said. Each morning, the first thing he did, or still does, was make a gratitude list. I haven't heard about gratitude lists in some time, but I used to hear about them all the time. So I forgot about gratitude lists, simply because the alcoholic is the great forgetter.   We forget everything that's helpful and remember everything that's harmful. It's a disease of forgetting, people in AA say.

The other stuff I've heard is mainly about having a Higher Power. Faith.
Faith that things will get better if I don't pick up / Faith that God has a plan for me / Faith that my current situation is only a means to an end, that things are *exactly* how things are supposed to be.

I struggle with God. But don't get me wrong, I do believe in one.
I believe that
> God is unknowable, unfathomable, beyond our mental limitations.
> God is shapeless. And what does shapeless look like?
> God is infinite, and I'm only finite. Which means I can't possibly imagine something infinite. I can't. It's simply impossible.

I can speculate, sure—and I love to speculate. Trust me I do. But speculation is only speculation. It's fantasies, and we all know what fantasies add up to:

A Waste of Time

But I just have to keep at it and my life will get better, they tell me;
and more will be revealed—or so they say.
Therefore believing in these sick sick sick people is a sort of Faith.

So I guess in a way I do have Faith. I have Faith in a *Group of Drunks*—now there's a scary thought....

G. O. D.

On the Bus

and We're Off....

1.

I'm sitting on the bus riding to Burlington to meet my mom who would in turn drive me to the house my parents had inherited from my deceased grandmother which I refuse to identify as a home.

My home:
- **Boston, MA**
- **Rutland, VT**
    ——Boston, moreover>>>>>>>>

So, while walking to the bus thinking I'm cut for time, I passed Hunter who asked What's up? and I said I was to catch a bus soon and I had to mosey on ahead so as not to be late. He said Where to? and I told him: To Burlington where my mom would in turn drive me to the house my parents had inherited from my deceased grandmother which I refuse to call a home (my only homes are stated above—in fact, I hate Stowe, VT, to tell you the truth) only leaving out the bit about my deceased grandmother thinking it was a given—someone must die for someone else to inherit their property—and Hunter said Huh, congratulations? not sure if he should be truly happy

for me, which I in turn followed with: Dude, someone
had to die for this to happen. He said Oh, and I said I'm
just kidding, dude. It happened about a year ago which
renders the inheriting of the house a good thing———
for my brother and sister and mom and dad, that is, but
not for me cuz for me it's a wretched little thing because
as a result I have not been to Boston this entire summer—people always die at the least convenient times if
you ask me

2.
Okay, so I'm on the bus.
Copies of my newest book *I Need Help: The SkullFuck Collection* came in the mail today, a big package on my porch
addressed to me; I'm reading A. M. Homes's memoirs, *The
Mistress's Daughter*, which I'm enjoying for the most part;
and I'm beating myself senseless, driving myself up and
down the wall, in putting together this new book called
The Lost Letters. Well, the madness began with *I Need Help.*
What pieces should I include? what pieces should I get
rid of? Or should I just say Fuck censoring myself even
if for the sake of page length and include it all?—which
is what I did end up doing, really. It's just driving me
mad cuz think about it: what, 8 books, 9 books, and I'm
going nowhere, receiving zero recognition for my hard
work—so I wonder what's the point, what the hell is the
point of all this? is that the point? ::: that there is no
point....

3.

Anyway, I'm on the bus, and it's taking us, the quiet, multicolored passengers, through a split in a large field that stretches as far as our eyes can reach, with sparse trees and bushes sprouting out of the grassy plains, but as the field unfolds, more trees and bushes spurt and push and take shape on the plains; and soon the mountainside, the overseer of where we are, looming neat and green and tidy above everything else, over-takes the plains to leave nothing but a shadow left be-hind.

After the books came in today, I went for a walk in search of Thurston, or Thirsty as some might call him, but I couldn't find him anywhere. I'm always running into him downtown, everywhere I go it seems at times, but to think when I actually need to reach him he's out of reach. Strange, right?

Cuz you see, I owe him a copy of *I Need Help* for allowing me to use his pictures in one of the pieces entitled "Hero or Vagrant?"—I also owe Fink and Mike, both of whom live in Boston, a copy cuz I used their pictures as well in the series entitled "Thicker Than Blood"; but Thurston, or Thirsty as some might call him, was the easiest of the three to track down since he lives right here in Rut-land—or so I thought.... Although not right here right now because I'm on the bus and what is here and now is the left side of East Bumfuck, just east of the Nowhere Meadows, where gay dudes, or faggots as some might call them, get together and drop drawers and dance pants-less as the sun goes down and the moon goes up and the man up there, straddling that silver sphere, looks down at the homosexual, pantsless disco and smiles.

4.
So I'm on the bus, going nowhere
So I'm sitting on the bus, writing nothing as the bus as-
cends and descends hills, jostles and bounces as it hits
bump after bump, and rocks and careens as the bumps
sideswipe the tires which makes it hard for me to type
cuz I'm sitting close to the back and back here the bumps
are bumpier and the drops are dropier, and the jostling
that takes place is like a jet plane in an epic surge of
turbulence....
I'm
not
really
sure
what
the point of this is, except
to kill time
and that's what I did....

5.
Anyway, I'm on the bus///

TONIGHT'S HALLOWEEN

I remember being 18 on Halloween and walking with Kristen to North Station where we would hop on the train to Salem, MA, for a wild Halloween night, and I would get blitzed and Kristen had to soldier-carry me all across Salem, trying to evade the swarming police that seemed to be lurking around every corner waiting to bust some heads—fun times, right?

Anyway, on the way to the train station, Kristen and I had decided on a story to tell people—because who needs a costume when you've got an excellent story to tell?—we decided that if anyone asked we'd claim

to be dressed as Sid and Nancy,
and this is not—I repeat, NOT—
the way we normally dressed,
even though it was, we just
liked to lie, so fucking what!
Nobody did ask anyway, or
maybe they did and I was just
too drunk to answer and Kristen was just drunk enough to
shout something like: Watch
out cuz I'll eat your fucking
kids!!!—and our awesome story
for the night never got told,
and so here I am, ten years
later, setting the record
straight about what had really
gone on all those years ago on
that one wild Halloween
night....

** ⌛ **

Tonight's Halloween and I'm in Stowe, VT—not Rutland
nor Boston where all my friends are probably getting
drunk or high right now, and probably getting set to
wreak havoc on their shitty old city—it deserves nothing less—but I'm here   in Stowe   heading to Burlington tonight, but   right now   I'm in Stowe   sitting
at the coffee shop writing in my thick notebook.
                    My dad had dropped me off
across the street, and as I had crossed, these two rubber-
necking girls, sitting in the front of their white SUV,

slowed down their mega piece of equipment and
watched me cross with wide, enquiring eyes.

They probably thought I assumed
they probably thought, *What a freak!* and they sat there
frozen in time as if just having seen a ghost, and then
the white jeep rolled farther down the road and it was
gone.

So this next bit is

only speculation:
I assume as the heat of the moment passed and they
were out of harm's way, it came to them at once and the
driver jammed her foot on the brake and the car skid-
ded to an immediate stop, as did the three cars behind
them, sliding on the pavement to make a black, zigzagging streak in the wake of the tires—and the car directly
behind the SUV tapped their rear bumper which gave
the two girls a jolting shove, their upper bodies flung
headlong but not hard enough to hit the dash—
and the driver straightened up in her seat, faced the
passenger, and said in a dumbfounded sort of way, Wait
a minute, it's Halloween ... I mean, *DUH!*—and she smacked
her forehead with the palm of her right hand, and then
reached out and ratcheted the stick shift and tapped the
gas and the SUV rolled forward and the stunned, angry
drivers sat in their cars aligned haphazardly on the
street, waving angry fists and grunting their groans of
disapproval———but it was too late to act, for the girls
were gone and it had happened too suddenly for anyone
to gather their license plate number.

!!!BACK UP!!!

Jeremy Void

Wait a minute, it's Halloween … I mean, DUH!—what the hell
does that mean anyway? that you *accept* my form of
dress today and only today?
But where was your acceptance yesterday? or the day
before? Honestly I'd much rather lose your approval
entirely than gain it for only one day out of the year—
Halloween, *please!*

I am pissing on your face right now don't you know?

Fuck the masses!
          what the hell do they know?
the mass fuckin public
carrying their fuckin vile
opinions of me——it's fuckin vile is what it is!

You take one of my eyes, I take both of yours.

You break one of my arms, I break both of yours
                and maybe even shatter your jaw while I'm
at it—for good measures I mean—to show you I do in fact
mean business:
DO NOT FUCK WITH Jeremy St. Chaos——————

Tonight I am not ~~Jeremy Void,~~ I am **Jeremy St. Chaos,**
although minus the real serious property damage, and
theft, and anything harmful toward others, for that
matter.

Halloween Night 2015

So then I guess I'm only Jeremy St.
　　　Chaos in theory
in talk
on paper and in writing—I can

cuss you out and do it well and get away with it in the
end because I don't give a fuck all what you think; your
thoughts mean nothing to me
　　　　　in theory, that is....

A Sex Inventory

A couple nights ago I went to read at the open-mike at the Turning Point Club. Everybody walked out of the room during my reading, and I received no applause.

Assholes!!!

Close to the end of the story I read, I heard a loud, obnoxious commotion coming from the hallway, a girl screaming about something or another. When I finished reading I could tell what she was screaming about. She was looking for an AA meeting; her dad was outside waiting to take her to one. They'd gone to the Methodist Church meeting on Williams Street, but apparently that meeting has closed for good. So they were at the Turning Point Club looking for another meeting.

A guy there was saying there's a meeting at the Trinity Church at 7:30. Being that I was pissed about nobody listening or even clapping, I thought I ought to go to a meeting, just to get out of there. So I asked for a ride to the meeting with her and her dad, and in return I'd show them the way. She said she'd ask him. I grabbed my leather jacket and followed her to the door. He said it was okay, and off we went.

Their dog was in the car with them, so I sat beside it. The girl thought it was really cute that the dog seemed to like me so much. Animals tend to gravitate toward me, for reasons I don't understand. There's just something about me that animals find appealing, I guess.

Anyway, we get to the Trinity Church ten minutes later. This girl seemed really nice, but crazy for sure, and hot. She seemed to like me too. I thought how great it would be to fuck her, since the last girl I'd fucked was Kristen and Kristen was probably out there fucking some other dudes right now. So it was about time I get some of my own, I thought.

This is the weird part:
So, this meeting we went to is the meeting in which only those who have completed the Steps the Big Book way are allowed to share. Which is the reason I'd never gone to that meeting in the first place. It's a Step meeting, which means every week they cover a different Step, all the way from Step One to Step Twelve, and then back to One. We were on Step Four that night, but I guess they divide Step Four into three separate parts since it's a long step:

Resentments   **Sex**   **Fear**

The section of Step Four we were on was Sex, oddly enough. So they discussed sexual conduct, how to treat women. It made me have second thoughts about having sex with this girl, because I decided a while ago that I was through with one-night stands. Having sex with this girl would only be that.

A Sex Inventory

On another note, there's one thing I don't understand about sexual conduct, and never have. Okay, they always say guys take advantage of girls, that they use girls for their own selfish purposes. I understand treating someone like a doormat or using them like toilet paper is wrong, but if the girl wants to have sex, is it really wrong to give her what she wants? Why is the guy always to blame in these situations? It's like, people complain that porn objectifies women, but what about the male porn stars? They're not being objectified? And they get paid less, too.

In our society, in our culture, it is always the guy taking advantage of the girl. And when I look back on it, I have taken advantage of some girls, but for the most part, they took advantage of me, and I only gave them what they wanted————is that so wrong?

Real Deviant Art

I'm so disappointed. I joined this site thinking it would be a great place to showcase my "deviant" art—art that deviates from the norm. That was before I learned that this is the biggest art site on the web. *Hmm.*

If it showed real "deviant" art, this would not be the case, because real "deviant" art is raw and offensive, or at least it is in my opinion.

But the opinion of this site differs from that: they consider all art to be "deviant" art.

Just the other day, a young girl by the name of Kaigan Spencer—otherwise known as BlackStatic-Kurone at deviantART—said this about one of my stories, "Love and Destruction":

> *"This is some of the most raw and real stuff I have read on [deviantART] in the six or so years of using this site. This writing, while quite intense and a bit hard to process at points, really makes it feel as if you're there with him having your brain wrung out wet-towel style as well. Not bad at all!"*

In a dialogue back and forth between me and her, beneath my brand-new poem "The Rage," these words were exchanged.

> **Kaigan:** *"Yep, know the feeling all too well."*

> **Me:** *"I used to be very angry and volatile, but I've changed my ways just slightly, and I'm trying to be more polite. Now, there's this woman who's a complete cunt, always bitching about her job. She's just a nasty, rotten individual.*
> *"Right before I wrote this, I had a dealing with her, during which I just nodded my head and said, Yes. I didn't actually say ma'am, but I'm sure you get the point.*
> *"So I know the feeling well because I was going through it at the time."*

> **Kaigan:** *"I remember trying to left hook a girl in my first three days of high school. Those were some fun times."*

> **Me:** *"Nice.*
> *"Yes, violence is funny, and what's even funnier is fucking*

with a bully or someone nobody ever fucks with because they're too scared to.

"I was out in the woods drinking around a bonfire with some of one of my ex-girl-friend's friends, back when I was eighteen and we were still going out. And there was this older guy who was a real prick and I saw him punch a younger guy in the face and the younger guy did nothing to defend him-self. When we were leaving and as I slid into my ex-girlfriend's car, she told me he forced him-self on her, and then I was back in the woods with a steak knife.

"When I stood before this big dude who was only about a cou-ple inches taller than me but many feet wider and a lot more muscular, I said something which I can't remember, and he got mad and threw his arm back, but I ducked away from his punch, sidestepped him, slid the knife out of my sleeve, and threw myself at him, knocking him over like I was some kind of rabid pit bull, and even after I lodged the blade in his thick neck, I continued to pummel

him. I got on top of him, punching him like crazy, as if he were one of those training balls that boxers used and would punch and punch and punch as it bounced and bounced and bounced and looked like a blur because the boxers would pound it so fast; and as my fists pelted him like hail, lightning-fast knuckles dropping on his face, I held the handle of the knife in my hand. The only reason he didn't die there was because I lodged the blade deep in his neck, which stopped the bleeding some.

"True store. I swear.

"The funny thing is, he was murdered a few years later; he was stabbed to death. I guess that's not so funny, just ironic."

Kaigan: *"Yep, you're definitely one of the most raw people I have seen on deviantART. Normally I expected people here to be quite tame, but that comment itself deserves to be featured somewhere."*

Again, thank you Kaigan.

I'm just so bored with the crap out there in this world, which is exactly why I'm making my own art. I just wish I could meet somebody like me, somebody who thinks like me, acts like me, blah blah blah—if only humans were created in my image. Reading poetry by similar-minded people offers me validation, shows me I'm not alone in this fucking world!

There's a quote by Andy Warhol that I really like, which goes like this: "Art is what you can get away with."

I have a different take on that quote though. <u>Art is getting away with something you wouldn't otherwise get away with.</u>

Art is supposed to be raw, it's supposed to push buttons. Because if it doesn't twist people's levers, I don't know, it just isn't that good. It's not daring.
I have the autobiography of one of my favorite writers, Richard Hell, and he talks about when he joined a poetry group in New York City in the '70s, and the group leader, one of his teachers from school, said to the whole group that the only one in this group who would get anywhere with their writing was Richard Hell, because his writing pushed limits, was risky.

He's my biggest inspiration and he has a poem describing in stunning details the act of masturbation. In his book, *Hot and Cold*, there are pictures of cocks and pussies. In the '70s he designed a shirt that said PLEASE KILL ME at the top and had a large bullseye across the whole front. He never ended up walking around Manhattan wearing it though, because he was too scared

to; but I know I would have in his shoes. I've walked around the city with even more fucked-up shit on my clothing than that.
I took a T-shirt and cut out two holes where one's tits would be and wrote across the front A PRODUCT OF A BUSTED CONDOM
and yes I wore it around Boston.

I got into a fight with these jocks at a Store 24 (a 24-hour convenient store in Boston) nearby the house I lived at the time, because the fat one was making fun of me for wearing a torn T-shirt that said FUCK ROCK & ROLL in really crass lettering.

The fat one paid for his hotdog and took it to the side to put it in the microwave, and when I finished paying for my items I looked over and saw the fat fuck stuffing his face with the hotdog, leaning against the counter and just munching on the wiener, like it was a fucking cock he was shoving into his mouth.
I said to the clerk working the register—*honestly, I really said this*—I said, Sorry about what I'm going to do.

The guy said something along the lines of, I understand.

I swiped my purchased items off the counter and headed toward the fat fucker standing by the door shoveling the heated wiener into his mouth. As I neared him I sucked a thick wad of phlegm up from inside me and I played with the nasty clump in my mouth to mold it into a better, more aerodynamic projectile for the situation.

Real Deviant Art

Then I approached him and I jerked my head back real fast and in an instant later, slammed it forward hard and let the loogy fly. It splattered in his face, in his eyes, on the nasty convenience-store brand hotdog—the fat fuck!

I joined my two friends outside in the parking lot, it was me and Chuck and Noah I think—followed by the fat fuck's black friend who when he eventually caught up to me slugged me in the face not once or twice but three times in all; but anyway the punches weren't exactly hard enough to knock me down.
I've been in quite a few different fistfights in my day, and I learned early on how to take a punch.
Plus, his hand probably hurt him more than it hurt me, because my head is hard as jewels. Seriously.

> I used to bash it
> off so many walls
> back in the day.

I didn't swing back though, not a single offensive move on my part. I just smiled and took it which I'm sure pissed him off even more.

You know,

> Once I got the shit kicked out of
> me and laughed the entire
> fucking time while the guy's
> fists were being driven into
> every inch of my face. I
> laughed and this made him
> even madder at me, and as my
> laughter and his anger both
> grew exponentially and the

blows kept coming one after
another, he started to swing at
me harder, which made me
laugh even harder; and he just
kept swinging with more and
more pummeling force but
nothing would get me to shut
the fuck up/

I kind of got lost in some war stories here, but the idea
is if it is real "deviant" art it takes chances and comes
from the heart, at least in my opinion. Real "deviant" art
is edgy and raw, it will surely piss you off, and most
readers will look at it or read it or whatnot and say, *He
doesn't know what he's talking about. He's just a fool for thinking that. An idiot. Cuz this can't be true*———real "deviant"
art is misunderstood by mainstream society because
they lack the ability to introspect.
That's why I listen to Punk rock, because Punk rock is
pure emotions, no techniques; there's no prior musical
experience necessary to play Punk rock. What makes a
Punk band good is the driving force behind the music:
> The singer's raw energy as he stalks the
> stage with the mike in his hand, the pure,
> unadulterated angst that seethes deep in
> his heart, the roiling pit of despair and
> frustration rising up and out his flapping
> maw as he howls into the microphone/
>> The guitarist's quick picking, his fast-
>> paced strumming—mostly down-
>> strokes for old-school Punk, but

newer Punk uses a combination of
both ups and downs—the energy of
his playing says a lot and really
brings the music to life/
    The bassist's cord progression
    simple and fierce, in sync with
    the guitarist's cord progres-
    sion, the speed and precision as
    he picks with one hand and
    climbs the fret board with the
    other/
        Then there's the Punk
        drummer, a rare breed,
        someone who needs to
        have a strong upper-
        body strength because
        he has to be able to drive
        the sticks into the drums
        quickly and rhythmi-
        cally—and I could never
        do it myself, honestly///
The original bassist of my old band Lethal Erection
didn't even know how to play bass when he joined the
band.

Punk rock comes from the heart—a heart soiled with
angst and frustration roiling through one's tormented
veins.
That's why I think *Hate* is an awesome thing; it gives you
a drive, a reason, a motive to act................

                   Anyway, I digressed

Termination Letter

To Mr. Therapist,

Friday night a friend told me that I'm the most tolerant person he knows. Why? Because he was having a really hard day and was being kind of an asshole, and even so I did not abandon him, I did not raise my voice at him, and I didn't even tell him once to mind his behavior. I just let him be a dick because I recognized that that's what he needed to do at the time; I recognized that he was in a bad mood, he was having a bad day, and everyone—including me and you—has those days, and trying to control someone in those states never ends good, because they're in a bad mood and their judgment is already skewed enough without me stepping in and trying to control them.

AA teaches me to have no expectations, to be loving and tolerant and forgiving, to accept people for who they are; and sometimes I fall short of those ideals because I'm human and I'm no different than anyone else—it's progress, not perfection.

That said, I have a lot of big changes coming up, what with me dropping to the most basic level of care in

Spring Lake Ranch's Rutland program, and I have said to you time and time again that I'm under a lot of stress.

And what do you do? You stretch the elastic, adding even more stress to what is already on its way to snapping, and then I get defensive, I get angry—how am I supposed to act in this situation? I mean, I just said to Steve on Thursday that we laugh at how stupid people react in times of stress in movies, when in reality we would react just as stupid, if not stupider, if we were in said character's shoes—so you yell at me, you raise your voice when you hit a brick wall, when you figure I'm not listening to what you have to say—which is ironic because when I feel like you're not listening to me I raise my voice too and you just pass it off as whining.
Ironic, judgmental, and very *very* hypocritical, to say the least.
This, from someone who prides himself on not being judgmental.

So I didn't show up to your appointment on Friday, I'll admit; I didn't respond to your first text, which asked me if I was coming in today, and I didn't respond to your second text, which said *Consider the implications of not responding to my texts,* or something like that. First of all, I didn't respond because I was already wanting to terminate our relationship, and figuring that wasn't the smartest thing to do right now, I didn't say anything at all. *If you have nothing nice to say, don't say anything at all.*

I met with Amanda later in the day and she suggested I text you just to let you know I'll be there on

Monday, and that I slept in late, which I told her I did, and which is entirely true, by the way. I wasn't planning on texting you, but as I considered what Amanda had said to me, I realized it would be the most mature and responsible thing to do. So I texted you, and in response you came at me with another angry text message, which mentioned Amanda herself, saying I contacted her but I didn't contact you; and which is extremely immature if you ask me, because Amanda has nothing to do with our issue and bringing her name into the conflict is completely unfair to her; it's so childish.

After I read that, I wasn't planning on responding to you at all. I realized that you care more about controlling me than helping me, and I wasn't going to satisfy you with a response. I already did the mature thing and texted you back, I already did the right thing—and you blatantly attacked me again.

But then I read the rest of the text message half an hour later and saw that you threatened to hold my meds hostage if I didn't do what you said—again, trying to control me and using whatever weapon you had at your disposal.

So I fired you. And I don't think I need to say anything else on that subject. Of course, you're gonna go to Dr. Fauntleroy and convince her of your side of the story, and make me look like the asshole, because that's what you do—you're convinced that you're right about everything and you spin it in your head in a way that makes you seem right to yourself and there is nothing I can say or do that'll prove this to you, because you are always right. You're the therapist and yet you lack the ability to introspect. How can you help anybody when you can't even help yourself????

So now I've gotta meet with you and Amanda and Dr. Fauntleroy on Monday to discuss how to proceed with my treatment from here on out, and whether I get my meds that day is completely "contingent" on how the meeting goes. So I—me and me alone—have no choice but to meet with three people who have worked together for years, who have heard your side of the story in advance but haven't heard my side of the story.
I can understand the need to include Dr. Fauntleroy in this ordeal, even though I don't agree with it since she deals with matters having to do with medication and this issue has nothing to do with medication; but I don't understand why Amanda needs to be included. From the looks of it, it seems like you're trying to hold her hostage too, as in if I stop seeing you as a therapist than I can't see her anymore either.

So on Monday I've gotta face the jury with nobody to vouch for ME, and you know, as I have explained time and time again, that I don't do well speaking, especially when I'm under pressure. You know this and still you find it necessary to set up this meeting.

I don't know if there's something going on in your life, outside of the office, that is effecting your ability to be a mature human being, let alone a therapist who deals with crazy people on a day to day basis—who, not to mention, can't handle when one of his clients acts a little defensive or erratic or whatever the hell you want to call it.

I know you've been spending all your free time at home building a garage or painting or whatever the hell you've been doing as of lately, and I can understand that must add a lot of stress to your own life—but if that's the case, I should not be seeing you anyway, because I hate to admit it but I go to your office for me.

Plain and simple.

I mean, I'm trying to do the right thing, everyfreaking-day I try to do the right thing, and I recognize that I'm not perfect and I never will be—it's a learning process and I still have a long ways to go—but this is my freaking life, and you're too busy playing your silly power games to see that.

An Art Exhibit

In Stowe, VT, right now and just tonight I attended an art exhibit at the Helen Day or Helen May or Helen Something, which is an art museum located right above the library.

It seemed less like an art exhibit and more like a discussion board about an upcoming art exhibit. Granted, there were three or four rooms adorned with various sculptures and painting planted here and there on the walls. None of it fazed me, really.

But for the majority of my time at the "exhibit" I sat around a square table gingerly drinking my coffee while the rest of the occupants, all older than me save for one who was maybe in his early twenties—even though I always identify myself with the younger crowd, which allows for the fact that maybe there were a couple people in my general age range, late twenties to early thirties, as I'm currently 28—they all sipped, or drank depending on how much their personal inner torment allowed for, glasses of wine and discussed the upcoming event.

> How are we gonna get more adults involved and/or interested?

what about children? should we get the
schools notified? offer events that cater to
the kids?

et cetera et cetera....

I admit that while this discussion went on around me
my heart was throbbing in my chest, pounding so loud I
could hear the fierce racking of it in my ears, feel it in
my bones, beneath my veins—the metronomic *thump!*

I listened though, and for the most part felt bored out of
my skull. This one guy was talking about his sculpture,
how they would go about getting it to the museum, since
it was so large and all. Others discussed what to have
happen while the sculpture sat motionless on display,
like should they put on a dance show? offered this one
woman who divulged that she was a choreographer.
This is where I myself chimed in: What about a poetry
reading? I suggested. You see, I went on, I like to read a
lot, but I don't read comic books—and I was killing myself for saying "comic books" as opposed to graphic novels cuz the sound of "comic books" must have made me
appear younger than I was, I assumed, but I carried on
anyway—because with comic books I flip through the
pages too quickly, since they're mostly pictures and I
have no medium with which to pace myself while reading them. But for "real" books, the existence of many
words allows me to stick around for longer.

So, a poetry reading would keep the consumer there, in
front of the sculpture, while the poem/story was being
read; it would keep them around, as opposed to having
them gaze upon the sculpture, either shrug or think to
themselves *Cool* or roll their eyes and think *Garbage,* and
simply walk away, as only seconds had elapsed.

An Art Exhibit

I said all this—but not in those exact words, for I stuttered, unsure of myself—I said all of it while my heart rate increased exponentially and the thumping in my ears became deafening, the pounding in my bones became painful and awkward, and when I finished up, I bowed my head, thinking to myself, *I never should have said anything.*

So, time went by, more discussion occurred, and I took to reading my own writing out of my sampler—as that was the only thing I had available to read at the moment—because the boredom and the anxiety persisted.

We gotta get more adults to come? we gotta appease to children too? notify their schools and whatnot? came from the crowd like a broken record.
                                   I mean, been there done that,
right?

So I raised my hand and volunteered, But what about teenagers? young adults? does anybody care about them?

And I received a room full of nods and silent agree-ments, for teenagers and young adults are important too, they said. But what do you suggest?
I went on to tell them about SPARC, about how the venue was intimidated by the police and the town and was forced to raise the fee, and as a result there was no more SPARC—
                        The only event in Rutland that
                        I know of which catered to
                        teenagers and young adults....

There needs to be more activity directed toward that age
group. Just for the sake of keeping them out of the
crushing grip of drugs and alcohol for a little while
longer. Granted, they'll probably just get high after-
ward, anyway. This is a given. But it's something, it's a
step in the right direction, is all....

I told them how the Chaffee Art Center in Rutland is so
generic, so commercial, and I got a room full of nods.
One woman piped in saying, But not in Stowe! No, it's not
like that in Stowe.
I wanted to say, Everyone likes to believe their art is not
generic, because it's their art, it's their children, and no
one likes to think of their children as regular, as boring,
they like to think of their children as special and
interesting, because it's their children, they raised
them....
But this is not always the case
although I kept my mouth shut on that point. Realized I
didn't need to point out the fallacy with "But not in
Stowe!"

So I pushed my concepts, and they listened, and as I
pushed, my heart rate settled, and I walked away somewhat at ease without shaking or fainting or worse. I
walked away unscathed and went outside to smoke a
cigarette. Halfway through my mom comes out and says
we gotta go get the pizza now.

In the car she said the guy in charge wants me to come
back and host a poetry workshop at some point
and I said cool

and we drove to pick up the pizza and went home, even though this isn't my home and never will be, it's just a mere substitute.

Ugh

Ugh
Another day of wasting away. Why bother? I keep saying. Why bother doing anything, its all the same. So I sit
here on my computer and tap out yet another rant to
add to the collection, but what for? What for what for
what for. I'm going nowhere, getting nothing, and I'm
burning out...

This energy will not last very long————
I'm surprised it's lasted this long

Ugh....
That's right——ugh....

Another day, another hour, another minute, another second, and I'm right here right now typing about another
nothing and what gives? It's all so pointless—yadda
yadda, blah blah blah, waiting again, and this patience is
killing me—blank and hopeless, running in a track of
dismay cuz it's all the fucking same....

So why do I do it?

Jeremy Void

Why not do it?
Why not do something else while I'm at it?
Another book, another chapter, another paragraph, another sentence, another word to fill in this pointless
rant about nothing and nowhere and it's futile so much
so why do I bother?

It's killing me—no royalties, no check in the mail; no
fame, no recognition, nobody even knows I exist ... what
the fuck?

I'm writing, it's pointless, I'm working hard, but it's
pointless, so why why why why WHY bother at
all?>>>>>>>>>
I'll tell you why:
                    I enjoy this kind of life I enjoy writ-
ing—words bring me joy and I'll keep writing till I die
                              regardless of
whether or not you like it because I'm not doing it for
you....
Or am I?

Why me, why this, why not that?
I need more, I need it, I need something that will lift me
up out of this shit————stick around cuz you know
what's going down....   Another pointless verse to fill
the page with....

AAAAAAAAAAAAAAAHHH!!!——   Go get fucked!

A Progress Report

It's been a rather busy night. I've been re-working my website massively, I emailed Jack Grisham from TSOL, in hopes that he will review one of my books, and that's about it, but I'll tell you I spent a hell of a lot of time on it.

A few days ago I took out all the individual pages that went with each book because there was barely anything on them, and created a community page that featured all my books instead.

But then I decided against that. I decided to remake the individual book pages, but this time add more detail along with the front and back cover and the small BUY ME sign. I added on each page, as well, a full table of contents with the pieces I made available for free in yellow and the pieces that are not for free and you can only see if you buy my books are in gray, ghostlike and fading away.

So I did all that—typing up the entire table of contents of each book and then going back and setting select pieces up as a link——— seven times in all.

So now I got that set up and I went to the homepage and realized that there is so much free crap available there that when the consumer finally decides to pull his/her head out of his/her ass and go on my site, he/she will be insanely overwhelmed by all the choices made available. As would happen to me if I visited your website.
So I deleted it all except for three pieces:

"A Bag Full of God"
                "with a hard-on for trouble"
                                "Verbal Acid"

saying that these are my favorites that I made free ("Verbal Acid" was newly added tonight so if you have not gotten your hands on my book *Just a Kid* yet and want to read the most mind-blowing of them all, a straight-up lobotomy done by an acid junky, sucking your brain out through a straw and tossing it in the grinder, you've gotta read this one—the words work like acid, and I'm still astonished by the astronomical fete I have reached in my writing),
and I followed it with a WARNING sign saying these pieces are racy so
BEWARE!

I started working on my website at maybe 11 last night and right now it's 5:30 in the morning.   See, I did a lot of work.

A Progress Report

I've been doing A LOT of work as of lately, as a matter of
fact.
Thinking about shit on a different level, writing shit and
enterprising shit, thinking of how to get my shit out into
the right hands, or the wrong hands whichever way you
wanna look at it. Either way I'm doing a lot and my
therapist is concerned that I'm gonna burn out soon. So I
said

> Hey hey Mr. Therapist, if I was
> gonna burn out I would have
> done it already, don't you
> think>>>>>
> I mean, for fuck's sake I
> wrote six decent fucking books
> in less than a year's time with-
> out burning out, and it didn't
> seem hard at all, it didn't faze
> me in the least bit.

The trick: NO SLEEP/
Although I only deprive myself of that necessary evil 2
to 3 nights a week, allowing myself to cool my jets before the next rush of energy that hits and comes surg-
ing out like a fountain of gism.

The other trick: MODERATION/
We could all do our drugs safely if only we could mod-
erate our fixes—but then what would be the point of
that? doesn't sound like much fun if you ask me—though
I'll tell you the moderation of sleep-deprivation isn't a
hard thing to do because halfway through the following
day my head starts to sink every hour, every minute,

every second, and then eventually just drops for good and I'm out for sixteen hours or so.

(I was thinking tonight that I eat for necessity but not for pleasure, I masturbate for necessity but not for pleasure, and finally I sleep for necessity but not for pleasure. Guess I'm just not a common dude after all— hahahah.
Well, at least I find that funny....))))

After I fixed my website all neat the way I wanted it, I went and emailed Jack Grisham from TSOL, and asked if he would review one of my books. Fingers crossed ...
or fingers crucified?
That sounds better, more like something I would say, a straight fuck you to the Holy Race, the ones who claim to be more than the humans who work and swarm like cattle every fucking day of their lives.
But no, the Catholics—or any Christian for that matter— are exempt from having to do it their way, exempt from the fucking Golden Rule (treat others the way you'd like to be treated).
Staring down through the holes in their snotty little noses, eyes to the sky, too good to look anyone in the eye, anyone other than the others who belong to the Catholic Race, who are made up with phonies and crack pots—
that's right, you're a phony!—your entire religion is based on the Roman government, don't you know?
Jesus Christ, he tried to take down the Roman government himself, but was arrested, tortured, and killed before he could succeed; and then these Romans who crucified the bastard, they wrote the fucking bible.

A Progress Report

¿WHY?

Well I'll tell you why:
Jesus Christ was an anarchist who despised money and
big businesses and all that crud; and was thus killed for
fighting for what he believed in, and the Romans took
the name of this great man, allegedly God's only son, and
did what all modern Catholics do—exploited him.

> Exploitation is the foundation
> of their entire religion, can you
> believe it!

And of course, all of what I said here is bullshit, I don't
really know what happened back then. I mean, how
could I? I wasn't even alive back then. Surely I could
take the word of a book written by an anonymous author who'd claimed to have spoken to God and God told
him what to write——and *that's* believable!

> (Anyone who made that claim
> today would be immediately
> deemed crazy and sent off to
> the loony bin.)

But I just feel like I'm better than that. I only trust
those who I know and respect, and I don't give a rat's ass
what the Bible says, anyway....

A Lowlife Scholar

"I'd rather be a king of nothing than a servant in a sick society."

— "Ain't Like You" by Blood for Blood

What's a lowlife scholar? A lowlife scholar is someone who ... um ... um ... a man who broke all the rules, lives on the run, didn't do well in school, and has a lot of fun. To me a scholar is someone who sits around smoking his corncob pipe and talks in a British accent to his friends, and complains about all the damned kids who come rolling past on skateboards—*damned kids!*

Scholars are boring; that life is boring—discussing philosophy over cups of tea and pipes of tobacco, puffing rings of smoke which float up and disperse into the air. Who would want to be that?

I'm a lowlife, a reformed lowlife, a loser in his own right. I lived a wild life, hung out with the homeless youth. It was fast, faster than racecars; it was crazy, crazier than the psychopaths put behind bars. I remember climbing out the window of a pickup truck while it pushed seventy miles per hour down the highway—all that just to retrieve a CD from the boom box I stored in back.

Girls, girls, and more girls, of course, was one of the perks of living wildly, living limitless (try jumping off a cliff and see where it gets you)—they surrounded me then, hung off of me like Christmas ornaments. They were everywhere, in my bed, the couch I slept on, the floor, and you bet, the tub too. I loved my girls and my women. And my drugs and my everything that comes with the fast-paced lifestyle I lived for so so long.

> *You see, I was a lowlife—I studied on the street, earned an associate's degree in refusing and rejecting the establishments, earned a bachelor's degree in resisting all conventions and traditions. Coasted right through the University of Going Nowhere, learned the lessons the hardest way possible—a couple of tough guys cornering me in an alleyway. That hollow* thud *of rugged knuckles being driven into the bare skin of one's palm, again and again—*smack! ... smack! ... smack! *The horrifying way in which these guys at the mouth of the alley are smiling greatly, grinning nefariously, eyes sharp and cunning, cold as a crisp icicle in February. Then there's that ominous feeling when you know you're alone and there's no way out and the only way through involves you getting your head slammed sideways into the brick wall. So you press your back to the brick wall behind you, feeling the abrasive surface scraping the skin just above your waistband, while your eyes dart this way and that, searching frantically for a solution, an escape route, a way out, but you know your fate all too well, you know it like you know the back of your own hand: these two*

guys who start in to the alleyway, advancing on you, closing in.

The guy on your right retrieves a cigarette and props it in his mouth. Flicks a Bic lighter and touches the flame to the butt. Puffs. Smoke streams through that cold-blooded grin of his.

He doesn't put away the lighter. He squeezes it firm in his grip, and then, as he gets nearer to you, he lunges forward, a charging step to gain extra momentum, and with the acceleration of his entire body his right first comes straight out and he smashes it through your face.....

I've been there myself; I've been punched and kicked and stabbed, and one dude even played basketball with my head. I've been beaten pretty bad, believe me on that.

But, as far as "real" schooling goes, a more conventional form of learning, probably even a more healthy mode of obtaining knowledge when I really think back on it—I found it rather boring, sitting in a classroom all day, behind a wooden desk, surrounded by my loud-mouthed peers who thought they were so damned tough, so badass, when all they really knew was the lame suburban streets they'd grown up on.

Me, I was picking up an education in the city. I was learning survival 101. From the best.

I was so busy with my unconventional method of learning that I just had no time for school, and be-

*sides, all that school ever teaches you is how to
follow rules, how to stand in line, how to be a
number.*
I am not a number, I am
not a robot, I am not a drone, nor am I a
mindless entity; *I refuse to follow your rules,
mainly because I have enough of my own.
But mostly because rules are stupid, boring nonsense only designed to keep people tied up.*

... tied down ...

   Bound
    Bound
     Bound
To what?

To *you?*

No, I would never be bound to you or what you stood for.
I was a rebel, through and through; a badass if
there ever was one. In Cuba the rebels are violent
guerrillas who will gun you down for nothing, that's
right—nothing. (But then, what else is there but a heaping pile of nothing?)

In America the rebels are different; we refuse to act and
dress and talk and be anything like you. That's my kind
of rebel. Not hippies, mind you. No, I was not a hippie,
because hippies are hypocrites and don't admit to it.

Me, I'm a hypocrite, only I'll admit to it.

A Lowlife Scholar

The other day I met a girl who I think I like—though I can't be too sure. I was showing her old pictures of me and one picture was of a friend of mine—not me—and his face had blood traversing it, lines of blood like open veins, and I told her I did it, I did that to him, it was me who did that to him, and it's true. I didn't tell her why, though. No I did not.

His girlfriend sucked me off in the bathroom and he found out so I said let's go outside, and as we walked out there, out into the cold, snow coming down hard and the ground slick with ice, I slid my hand in my pocket and fetched the lighter I used to light my cigarette. Squeezed it firm in my hand, so that ... you'll see.

We went into the alleyway and he took the first swing of course, but his feet caught on the ice and he slid and his feet slipped out from under him as I lunged on top of his fallen body—he was a big guy too, a real big dude— and I sent my fist packed with my lighter down on him, punch after punch after punch, every inch of his face, my knuckles shoved into his cheek, his eye, his nose, his forehead, bam bam bam, got you sucker, and his skin split—it must have hurt.

But we made up later because we were close friends— only I was an asshole and I do feel bad for how I acted, but I can't take it back no matter how hard I wish it.

Oh yeah, what was I talking about again?

A lowlife scholar, I guess.

Well, I think I answered your question. Did I not?

A lowlife scholar is me. So you can take your useless piece of paper, administered by a college that cost a fortune to get into, and shove it up your ass!

> *I don't need your approval, I don't need you*
> *measuring my level of intelligence by what a piece*
> *of paper says—because after all, I did write three*
> *books, which is much better than any of you ass-*
> *holes could do.*

In the end, all I really want to be is me, and if that means being a lowlife until I die, then good riddance.

So save your judgments for someone who actually cares.

Sunday Brunch

I went to a small party today. It was supposed to be a brunch, I was told, although it started at 1, which to me seems kind of late for a brunch. More like lunch.

And plus, the food served there seemed much more upscale than that of a brunch. Usually, I know brunches to have breakfast food, as opposed to steak and stuff like that———
although the food was delicious I must add. Tommy I----
brought these jalopeño something-or-others, which were really good. I wouldn't have eaten them otherwise, but out having a smoke Tommy asked if I like spicy food which led to him telling me about those jalopeño things, whatever they're called, and I told him I'd try them; and I'm glad   that I did>>>>>>>>>>>

Good people there too. Nice people. People I met at the open-mikes I frequent.
....The Regulars ::::
There were
- Dennis
- Rebecca
- Tommy I----
- and a woman named Lori who told me she was Maggie K-----'s mom

It was hosted by Corrina S------- and Mark C--------.
I've known Corrina for some time now,
though I can't say where I met her.
I met Mark maybe a few weeks ago at Pub
42 on a Sunday night.
I guess he and Corrina had gotten back together or
something some time prior and after Corrina introduced the two of us he did the gentlemanly thing and
bought a copy of my first three books to give to Corrina.
(That's right, it's gentlemanly to buy MY books for your
girlfriends——get that through your head.)

Last Sunday they had a "brunch" too, at which Corrina
and Mark had shared some of my writing with their
guests, and I was told later that night at Pub 42 that they
enjoyed what they'd heard, and this led to Corrina inviting me to the brunch the following Sunday—
which happened today.

I had a good time there.
I'm not usually much of a social person, but I thought
What the hell, I'll give it a shot...................
Yes, I found myself bored at various stages of the party,
but that's a given any time I find myself in the company
of others.
(I find that for the most part people bore me, which says
more about me than it does about them.)
But all and all, I'm glad that I went.

You see,
I'm not very good in the company of others; I don't know
how to act properly cuz over the years I've never really

learned. Parties in the past have always been loud and
rambunctious, and nobody ever acted "properly"—
                    well, in a way I guess we did,
                only our standard of acting "properly" was
                very different than the standards of most
                others.

But I do want to get better; I want to learn how to act
properly because I want to go somewhere with my writing and in order to do so

I must learn how to deal with other people
I must learn proper social protocol...........................

                                    So I went,
                              and like I said,
                        I'm glad that I did..........

                    **   ⧖   **

Anyway, I was thinking about something, which turned
into a long digression about the party—a long introduction to put the groundwork in place.
                    I was thinking about the con-
cept of "fashionably late."
You see, I'm a very punctual person; I've never been big
into following trends and thus never cared for being
fashionably late.
                    If a party starts at 1,
                you'd assume it started at 1, right?
But no,
most people take their time to get there,
for various reasons, I assume....

Jeremy Void

They have to get dressed, look right,
they have to do their hair up all neat and pretty,
they have to apply makeup to cover their moles and zits
                                    and proof of old age,

and guys have to wait for their girlfriends or wives to
        do all this
and maybe some guys like to dress up nice too
                                    who knows?

Me,
I just went in whatever filthy clothes I was wearing at
the time, and to think,
I thought *I* was late......................................
                        I was late according to the
rules of anti-fashion, I suppose.
I was a good thirty minutes late, and I was even nice
enough to send a message via Facebook to let Corrina
and Mark know I was on my way.
But I was the first one there—so weird—which put me
under the impression that I was the only one invited, or
at least the only one who could make it anyway....

Then another half an hour went by before there was a
knock at the door. Tommy I---- and Lori K------ were
right outside. A little later came Dennis and Rebecca.

I will never understand people. Why is it cool and
acceptable to be late? It's like, you want everyone to already be at the party when you get there so you can
make an entrance or something.
                        I don't know

It just seems so odd. Pointless, really. But then, I'm rather odd myself and everything that seems odd to me is actually normal to most people. Normalcy is so strange and I'm glad that I'm not that way——I'm glad that I'm odd.

Anyway, I had a good time there. Thanks, Mark and Corrina, for inviting me....

206

The Crazy Ward

1.

True story:

I remember a time in the Crazy Ward being followed down the hallway by the doctor who holds a clipboard in his hand and he's asking me questions and I refuse to answer and I'm all loopy on Librium, that strong benzoate they give people for alcohol withdrawals, you know the one\
But anyway, I'm loopy and my feet follow the floor in a sort of zigzagging formation, and I sway one way, and then another, back and forth, all the way until I reach the room I was assigned to, and when I get there my feet catch on one another and I twirl straight down to the ground, just unravel like a ball of yarn, landing flat, smack, on my back>>>>>>>>>>
Then the doctor says to no one in particular,
just speaks the words to the air as
they fade into oblivion
he says, "Throws himself on the floor for
attention"
and he looks at me with these mean green eyes, clearly the eyes of a temptress, a fisherman sending his bait across the sky and into the lake
and I catch it in both hands and say

I say sneering
I look him square in the eye, my own eyes pointed and
fierce, mean and volatile, with the edginess of an axe
murderer
I say, "You wanna see me hurt myself for
attention?!"
and the doctor looks me over, with a grin that says *Don't
you dare!*

I stand up on uneasy feet and return the glare/
I return it even harder
and a One ... and a Two ... and a one-two-three-four/
I lunge head-first into the wall
just like that
my hard head connecting with the wood and plow-
ing straight through, leaving a hole the size of ...
well ... my head >>>>>>>>>>>>>>
"SECURITY!!!" the doctor shouts out the door.

Before long a crew of security guards of all sizes and
creeds flank me from every single angle; they sweep me
off my feet and drag me into the silent room. They
throw me in and lock the door.
I pace
I'm angry
the anger growing on me like a sick-ridden boil
the rage roiling from my heart
to my head
all over
everywhere
and I continue to pace,
my arms looped messily behind my back
I pace

keep pacing as if
     this song is set to repeat itself.

Then the door flies open, and I whip my head toward the
opening and in comes the doctor, flanked by two tough-
guy security guards, almost like thugs standing there to
protect their boss.
They all have expressions on their faces that state rather clearly
     Tsk tsk tsk........................
         and
     Do not fuck with us!

But I'm not scared—not at all—no I'm fuckin not
cuz the adrenaline has seized me
flashes of a fierce, electric anger rushing
     through my veins
my mind racing, my body overtaken
by a hysteric kind of energy that has been
     locked inside my brain
         holding me tight until
           I fuckin explode——
at this point there is no turning back
at this point I'm in it for the long haul
at this point my mind is made
     the following set of actions could not
         be changed by anyone
         cuz the way I see it
THERE   JUST   IS   <u>NO TURNING BACK</u>

The security guards hurry into the room
         a total onslaught of muscles and bronze

They grapple me, twist me around, and steer me straight
to the bed. But me, I'm completely out of control. I don't
go without a fight. My arms swing as they each grip one
of them, my legs kick as they try to hold me steady. But
I'm too nimble to be kept in place. I flail and thrash,
they wrestle and grab.
They're stronger, a lot stronger than I am, but me, I'm
quick and slippery—I squirm in their holds.
The two guards grapple me and drag me to the bed,
           hoist me up and toss me on it as though I'm
           just a mere piece of trash and my well be-
           ing means nothing to them.
But I'm stark raving mad
      and
           I refuse to give up fighting
                  not now
                  not ever....
They tie the straps around my wrists and
      there's just no getting out
                  not now
                  not ever....
I scream and I shout,
      rattling my wrists in their cage
      kicking my feet up and down
and the braces bang and thwack against the bedframe

but it's to no avail; it's so utterly hopeless by this point.

Finally realizing I'm firmly braced to the bed, they leave
me alone now...................................

                  Thoughts of despair
                    and hopelessness

flash through my head
like a film reel showing me
everything in this world
that I don't really wanna see.

Now,   I'm scared—fear starts to set in as I evaluate my
predicament, strapped down to this bed in the silent
room of the Crazy Ward, with no escape, no way out, just
me and my own rampant thoughts———cuz you see, I've
never been restrained like this before.
Sure, I was committed when I was a child, for smoking
weed and having both suicidal and homicide tendencies
and ideations; but back then I was almost a saint. I had
dark thoughts, sure, but I was too frail, too anxious, to go
and act them out.
I was a good boy then.   Remember, this was when I
was only fourteen-years old, and I went in almost a saint
and I came out a fucking monster————this is what
your unbreakable, incorruptible system had done to
me—a system you think so highly of///

Anyway:
Some time later, the nurse, an Indian woman with a
small red dot on her forehead, gently opens the door,
looks me over for a moment, standing gingerly in the
doorframe, and then ambles through the opening. In
one hand she carries a clear plastic cup containing two
pills, in the other a small Dixie cup filled to the top with
water.
                    She approaches the bed and says rather po-
                    litely

she looks down at me with these nice, pleading eyes, like
she's only doing her job and she could care less whether
I take them
        she holds the pills and water above me and
        says, "Would you like to take these orally?"
and I instantly kick both cups from her hands and water
splashes in her face and down her scrubs and the two
pills plummet to the floor.
        With no regard whatsoever I spit out
        in my meanest voice ever I shout at her, my
            voice carrying the sharp, preciseness
            of a sledgehammer coming down and
            breaking through blocks of concrete
        I give her the hardest stare I can produce
            and say in my nastiest voice
        I spit, "And remove that fuckin dot from
        your fuckin forehead, you fuckin dune
        coon."

——————As if on cue, in come the doctor and the
doctor's two thugs and out comes the needle. He holds it
straight facing up, out in the open so that I can get a
clear view of it, so that I understand what's going to happen to me, so as to teach me a lesson, I suppose.
Like I said, I'm scared/   No, I'm rather horrified.
I have no clue what the hell is going on ...
    what the hell is going to happen to me/
           There's a first time for everything
                I guess///

And I'm flailing as the thugs grab me there, unstrap the
brace restraining my right wrist, flip me easily onto my
left side as I try to fight back but to no avail, and I can

feel my pants being yanked down past my asshole, and I
can feel the pinch as the needle slides into my skin, slic-
ing through one of my ass cheeks, and I can feel the needle being slipped out of me, and then, almost immediately, I can feel my conscious slipping, my eyes drifting,
my head getting heavy, my whole world going liquid,
everything fading—lights, structures, shapes, everything—all of it going dark, dark, dark
and out go my lights as my head plops on the pillow and.

For the whole weekend I'm out cold.

I remember three things and three things
only about that weekend:
1. I spilt soup on my lap
2. I screamed that I needed safety pins
3. And the doctor let me phone Kristen—who had
   driven down from the Cape to visit me in the
   hospital the Friday night I was restrained—so that
   I could explain what happened, say I'm sorry,
   etcetera.

I woke up Monday morning, feeling a little woozy, and
the doctor led me out of the silent room to my bed in the
Crazy Ward proper.

2.
True story:
I say to the nurse, who had just handed me
a cup filled with this thick, black
syrup that resembles charcoal and
kind of tastes like it too, I remember

from me previous visit to the crazy
ward
(they give it to patients who've taken a large consumption of pills; it absorbs the drugs so that they don't die
from an overdose)
"If I drink that shit, I'll puke," I say to her
she leaves the room then and comes back with a square-
shaped bucket
she hands it to me and says, her voice
tinted with snobbines, as if I'm here
and she's there but she couldn't care
less about me—it's late at night and
she just wants to get this over with
and go home and pass out on her bed
she says, "Puke in that," and walks out the
door and leaves me to my own devices.

So what do I do? I tip the cup upside-down and pour it
out entirely into the bucket. When she comes back I tell
her that it's all my vomit, and she shrugs and takes it
away.

Let me back up for a minute. How'd this night start?

*Earlier tonight I had come home from work in a shit mood, after
a shit day at my job——I was so fucking pissed ...*
so sick of my nagging boss, the complaining
customers who bitch relentlessly about this and that: the pizza
wasn't hot enough, the soda wasn't cold enough, the tables and the
chairs were sticky with residue from the previous diners to
have sat there. One of the customers even complained that I was
mopping the floor ...
The Fucking Floor! *no joke*

The Crazy Ward

Can you believe that shit?

Anyway, amid the rage that festered
in my head, I slammed through the
front door of my house, and my
mom shouted "Jeremy!" as I rushed
up the stairs to the second floor.

I know exactly where my mom hides the K-pins I take every sin-
gle morning for my social anxiety, I thought to myself as I
stomped up the stairs, because I'd stolen them before.   (The
doctor had only agreed to prescribe them for me on the condi-
tion that my mother holds onto them and hides them.)

I threw open the door to her bed-
room, headed straight to her
dresser.

I yanked open her dresser drawer
I snatched up the clear, orange bottle
I popped the cap, tipped it back, and let the orange pills
                               roll easily down the hatch.

Not the best place to hide them I have to say.

The door barged open then, and
there stood my mom, just outside of
her bedroom.

"Jeremy, are you okay?" she says.

I didn't say a single word.
                I just hurried straight past her.
                               I didn't say a single word
                               as I descended the steps/

and headed out the front door and hopped inside my minivan
and started the engine. I cracked one of the six beers that I had
bought at the liquor store before driving home.

> *I drank a total of two or three, be-*
> *fore the cops stopped me, had me*
> *pull over, and cuffed me in the*
> *backseat of their cruiser as I waited*
> *for the ambulance to arrive and*
> *take me to the hospital to be evalu-*
> *ated by a doctor. Guess my mom*
> *had phoned the police after I had*
> *taken all those K-pins.*

So, the nurse comes back into the room and takes the
square-shaped bucket filled with the charcoal-like substance away from me and leaves me alone in the care of
a security guard who sits in a chair just outside of the
room.

I sit on the bed and wait
I have nothing better to do right now
        other than wait
I check the clock which
                ticks and tocks on the wall
a steady, relentless sound that drives me
                        even crazier than I already am.

The time is irrelevant though, cuz who knows how long
it will take for the doctor to show up and evaluate me?

        Finally he comes in to the room, the
same doctor who had evaluated me the last time I had
been committed———

<u>the instance mentioned above</u>
A short, thin man with a pair of nerdy-looking glasses
set evenly across the bridge of his nose, he looks kind of
Asian, but not enough to tell for sure.

He sits down in a chair
I sit on the bed, my legs dangling over the side.
        He looks me square in the eye and says
I could tell he's calculating what to say; his demeanor
seems even, as if he's in charge of the situation, as
though he has me
but he does not
        he says, "Why did you take the drugs?"
        "Cuz I was angry," I say
        he says, "Why were you angry?"
        "You really wanna play this game?" I reply
        "Just answer the questions," he says
        "A bad day at work. I just needed something
        to take the edge off, is all"
        he says, "You took half a bottle of Klonopins"
        I nod
        he says, "But why? Were you trying to kill
        yourself"
        I shake my head
        "That's an awful lot," he says to me
        smoothly. "Why?" he says again. "Don't you
        think just a few would have been enough,
        would have generated the same effect you
        were looking for." Pause. "Were you trying
        to kill yourself?" he says again, as if not
        hearing me the first time
        "No," I say to him. "No, I wasn't"
        he says, "Are you afraid of the future?"

"No"

"Are you sure about that?"

"Of course I am!"

I cross my arms and look away from him, off to the
right and out the door

he says, "Have you ever been to China,
then?"

"No," I say again, like a damn broken record.
"No, I haven't"

he says, "Then why not?'

"Um ..."

I think about it. Why haven't I been to China?

"I have no desire to go," I say finally

"Is it because you're scared?"

"No"

"Jeremy, is it because you're scared?"

"No. I told you already I'm not scared"

"Jeremy?" he says coos, like a lover trying
to get my attention

"What?"

He stands up

he looks down at me and says, "That's all I
need to know," and then exits the same way
he came in—through the door, the only way
out.

I sit there and mull over what just happened. *China?*
What the fuck!
Why the hell would I ever want to go to China? I don't even like
Chinese people, they give me the creeps.

So I push myself to my feet and rush the door.

I reach it and I scream as loud as I can

        I wave me fist and raise my voice as I holler
        through the door, "Hey! HEY!!!"
this catches the security guard's attention
           he looks up at me and says
           he sits there in the chair and looks at me
           and says, "Keep it down, will you!"
           "Fuck off!" I snap. "Hey!" I repeat. "Hey, come
           back here. I wanna talk to you, for fuck's
           sake. Fucking come back her!!!"

I wave my fist as the security guard stands up and gets
in my face.
Chest to chest now, "Shut up, there are other people
here," the guard scolds.
           "Move!" I shout. "Get out of my way!"
           "No!" says the guard. "Get back in the room
           and sit down!"
he punctuates his point with a thick index finger direct-
ing me back into the room
           "Move!" I shout again. "FUCKING MOVE!!!"
           "Hey!" he says. "Watch your mouth, there
           are other people here"
           "MOVE!!!"
He shoves me backwards, hard
into the room.
I cock back my arm and nail him right in the nose
He pushes me back and knocks me down. Grapples me as
I fight back.
More guards mob the room then. I can't see the guard
that I decked anymore as a mass of guards surround me.
I'm fighting, and they're leading me right to the bed.
They hoist me up and lie me down

they strap me in—all but one wrist, my right one—so that they can easily push me on my side and poke me with the needle, which is exactly what they do.

As the guards exit the room I catch sight of the one that I decked in the face and a thick line of blood oozes from his nose.
At that I feel quite satisfied.

I lie there, feeling proud of myself, as the tranquilizers kick in.
> (At some point that night they
> even shot me up a second time,
> which only heightened the
> chances of an overdose, but I
> can't remember the order of
> events and what provoked the
> second shot, so I'll show only
> one in this story.)

I'm thinking to myself, *They might have won the war in the end, but I had dealt blood—actual blood!*
I look down and see splotches of blood splattered on my shirt.
At that I feel quite satisfied.

They might have won the war in the end, but I had dealt blood—actual fucking blood!
Score one for the crazy man.

I lie there feeling so so so satisfied for my rein of terror when the feeling of having to pee creeps into me.

I shout, but not too loudly, as I'm finally
      wearing down from all the sedatives
      I have consumed that night
I shout, "I have to pee!"
ignored
      I shout, "Come on, I have to fucking pee!"
ignored again
      I repeat, "I have to pee!"

Finally, a young woman, clearly a nurse in her blue
hospital scrubs, comes in and places a plastic cup over
my groin and then leaves me alone again.

      "What the hell am I supposed to do with
      that?"
ignored
      "Can't you see I'm strapped in here?"
ignored again

Fuck it, I think to myself.   *FUCK   THIS!!!*

I wiggle my right hand, making it as thin as can be, and
with much effort, slip it out of the strap and swing it
over to my left wrist and unstrap it manually. I sit up
and lean over to reach my feet and unstrap those ones
too.
I kick my feet to the floor and start for the door. At this
point I'm too zonked to make a scene, to put up a fight, I
just casually leave the room and walk to the bathroom
and enter. I drop my drawers and fire a line of piss into
the toilet.
I exit the bathroom and a different security guard is
standing there, I assume because I claimed the other one

had laid his hands on me first and to be safe they've removed him from the picture.

This one though, he puts his hand lightly on my shoulder and directs me to the room. This might only be the
drugs talking, but his touch feels almost fatherly against
my skin: serene, safe, as though I can trust him.
I walk beside him and enter the room and lie down on
the bed without putting up a fight, my eyelids and my
head quite heavy already, getting ready to drop as I slip
into oblivion. He straps me into the bed and this time
wraps Duct tape around the braces

> and he says to me then, "I've worked here 12
> years, and I've never seen anyone get out of
> a 4-point restraint, so this time I'll keep
> quiet about it. But if you try that Houdini
> shit again, you're never getting out of here.
> You hear me?"

I nod
as blackness immerses the guard and my conscious flees
as I ease into a deep, heavily-drugged sleep.......

When I finally wake up I'm in the Crazy Ward proper///

We Live and Then We Die

People are so afraid of the truth. I was with a friend a month or two ago and I needed cigarettes so we went to the Walgreens a few blocks from where I live, knowing that they take EBT (food stamps/cash benefits) so I could buy my cigarettes with that since I was broke otherwise. So I'm standing in line waiting to step up to the register and order my cigarettes when I turn to my friend and say rather loudly, somewhat belligerently, with the hope to annoy the bystanders, I said, "Isn't it great how we live in a country where the government will simply give me free money just so I can go kill my-self." This of course provoked many sorts of sneers, from the classic variety of screwing up one's face, to rolling one's eyes, to crossing one's arms, looking up, and looking down through one's own nose. But why? It's so very true. So my turn comes up and I order my pack of smokes, and the girl at the register's nose is wrinkled and pruned as she scrunches up her face and looks at me in utter contempt. I see her glare, look at my friend, who I can tell also sees her glare, and he nods and says, "And thank God for that."

"God bless America," I chuckle, pay the girl, pocket my smokes, and walk away laughing.

What's so offensive about that? Like, today, at the bakery I got this hefty chocolate pastry and when it came my turn to order I pointed down into the display case at one of those pastries and said, "One of those chocolate tooth-decays, please." No one heard my remark though, nobody that I could tell, anyway. "A chocolate croissant?" she said. And I nodded, "Yeah."

Life is a joke if you ask me. Life is ugly, life is rotten, life brings all batches of disappointment when you least expect it, and when you do expect it, it gives you something you don't expect, something even worst, like a kick to the nuts when you had expected a punch to the face. That's life for you. It's a terrible terrible thing, and yet, I haven't died yet, I'm still here, and I refuse—simply refuse—to go on living with my head in the sand, a passive bystander who gets slapped in the face, smiles through the pain, and says, "Thank you, may I have another."

NO I CANNOT DO THAT.

It's not in my DNA to sit back and let life happen to me; I must make it happen, I must stand up and take charge and kick some fuckin ass, cuz if I don't life will kick my fuckin ass....
                    Not That It Hasn't Already

So——my point is life's a joke. Why take yourself so seriously? Why mope all day when I can go around making jokes out of my own misery. I'm not the kind of person who goes around smiling all the time because life is so awesome that I would marry it and fuck it, and I would fuck it hard, so hard cum will be spraying outta me like from a water hose. That's not how I live my life. I'm honest and blunt, I'm innocent and bright, I'm lucid and slippery and I'll make you shiver the next time you see me. A liquid quiver running down the length of your spine, an electric tingle so vivid and visceral it will make you happy and sad and glad that you're a man (or a woman), it surges up your spine at the same time. That's me, I'm lyrically inclined to blow your fuckin mind.

But the thing is, the problem is, the issue I'm having is— —people do not appreciate it like I do. People don't want the truth, they want a fabricated reality. They don't want to make art, they want to use other people's art.
              The Only Real Artists We Have in This World Anymore Are Rip-Off Artists

We all live and then we die. I won't tell it any other way....

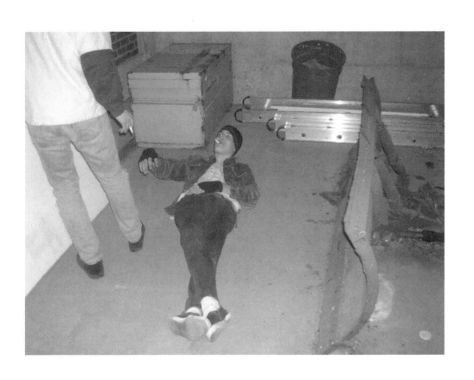

Fucking Pissed

I'm really fucking pissed right now. My dad's been pushing me to get the flu shot for weeks now, and when I told
the guy that's crashing with me for a very short period
of time that I've gotta get the flu shot, he jumped at the
chance to voice his opinion. My dad is misinformed, he
said. He probably only reads billboards and watches
commercials on TV. Now, *that* really got me going.

   As we walked to the AA meeting together, I
asked him how many people does it take to argue, and he
wouldn't answer; so I kept pressing. Eventually I got him
to say two, or maybe I said two and forced the words in
his mouth, I don't know.

I explained to him that there are two sides to every coin;
and he denied it. I told him that what happens is both
sides dish out their facts, and it's up to us as the consumer to choose a side, to choose which facts to agree
with, to choose which facts *not* to agree with; and he denied it. I explained that our culture is based on this
principle, the principle of propaganda; and still convinced that he's right, he denied it.

So I asked him where did he get these so-called "facts,"
and he wouldn't answer.

   He said there's so many places.

I said tell me one.
He said I don't know where to start.
Just one, I said.

Finally, I got him to spit out the World Health Organization. So I asked if he did the research himself. He said yeah, I read all about it. I said no, did you yourself put the flu shot under the microscope.

Then he said but they have nothing to gain.
I asked how do you know?
He said what could they gain?
I said there's *always* something to gain.

Don't forget, this whole time I'm shouting at him, because he's being so fucking stubborn. I hate when I challenge someone's opinion, someone who claims to know the "facts," and they give me vague answers in response.

He even said to me, If you seriously want to argue about this, I'll blow you away; you'll be shocked at all the stuff going on out there.
Yes, that's exactly what I want to do:
ARGUE. In fact, I want to argue about this so badly that I've been trying to pull you into an *argument* for the past ten minutes.
.............*FUCK.....*

But when we got to the meeting I realized I've been overreacting about this whole thing. He has a right to his opinion, regardless of how little information he has to support his claim.

So I went over and apologized, quietly because the meeting was just getting started. Then I sat down, pulled out my phone, and sent him a text message:

Let's just agree to disagree, okay?

In response to that, he said I'm just trying to help you, you really shouldn't get that shot, blah blah blah.

ARE YOU FUCKING KIDDING ME!!!

So then I grabbed my notebook from my bag and started writing.
Does anyone have any ideas?

My Story: The Short Version
Remastered

Certain AA meetings feature speakers, who usually tell their stories for the first half of the meeting, while the second half of the meeting is designated for discussion based on and inspired by the speaker's story. For some speakers, they know they are to speak months in advance, and some only find out the day of. For me, I knew months in advance and thus had time to plan out what to say. The only other time I spoke was at an all men's retreat, and instead of telling my own story, I read a very gruesome fictional piece I wrote, but although it was entirely fictional, it very accurately portrayed the feelings associated with addiction and alcoholism, because that I do know first-handedly.

But for this upcoming meeting at which I was to speak, I chose to tell the truth—as best as I could at the time—and, figuring that writing is the strongest, most powerful weapon at my disposal, prepared a story in advance. This is that story—it's entirely true.

I do hope someday to stretch out this story, but for now, this is all I've got.

** **

I don't like to talk about the good
deeds I do, because I feel like talking about them would
cause people to say,
  "Hey, Jeremy, you are so awesome for having done that;
                you are the greatest person alive,"
and I feel like having people admire me like that would
do more harm than good. It would only serve to boost
my ego, and for an alcoholic that's a terrible thing to
have happen.

  But there's one instance that I talk about quite often—ask my sponsor, and he'll tell you all about it—because this particular instance was a mind-blowing
experience and I feel as if the telling of it might help
others step up and do the right thing too.
                It happened three years ago. I
                hung out most the night with
                my ex-girlfriend, who wasn't
                my ex at the time, in her
                hometown of Beverly, MA. I
                myself used to live in a sub-
                urbs just outside of Boston, MA,
                called Newton, where my par-
                ents still live today. That
                weekend, I was in Boston visit-
                ing friends and family and I
                was staying at my parents'
                house in Newton.
                It was between ten and
                eleven PM when I got on the
                commuter rail back into the
                city. On the commuter rail, sit-
                ting in the row across from me,

was a kid about thirteen- or fourteen-years old, crying his eyes out. And there were these douchebag jock types sitting in the row in front of him turning around and leaning over the seat to point and laugh at the "cry baby."

I called the kid over to me and he sat down beside me, hiding the tears in his eyes with his hands, and I asked him what was the matter. He told me. He lived in Maine, he was lost, somehow having made it to Boston, and he didn't know how to get home. His cellphone was dead too, so calling his mom was out of the question. He was basically screwed. So I said he could use my cellphone to call his mom; he called her, and they talked for a bit, and then I told him I'd help him get home. Which I didn't have the power to do myself. So when the train rolled into North Station, the last train stop on the line—North Station is a subway station in Boston, for those who don't know—I walked the young boy off the train and brought him to the subway security.

The guy I dropped the kid off with was kind of a jerk to us, acting like both of us were stoned and were only pulling his leg or something, but in the end he agreed to take the kid from me and help him get home.

Still, I was nervous. When I arrived back at my parents' house in Newton at around midnight, I called my girl-friend, panicking, thinking I had just screwed the kid over. You see, I didn't trust cops or security guards—and I still don't—and I especially didn't trust the security working for the subway system. So my girlfriend suggested I call his mom the next day, since he called her on my phone and so her number must have been saved in my phone.

I didn't end up calling her the next day, but I did call her the day after that. I still re-member the setting of the phone call. My dad had driven me back to Vermont earlier in the day and the two of us went to see a movie before he would leave and go back to Boston. I don't remember what movie it was and I don't remember how I decided to call her during the movie, except that I did call her. I stepped out to have a smoke during the movie and I called her.

He made it home safely, she said, and she was absolutely thrilled with me. She was so grateful. She asked for my name and took down my number so her son could call me himself, and my phone rang while I was in the theater and I stepped out and answered. He was just as grateful, if not more. We talked shortly, and I told him he could feel free to call me if he ever wanted to talk about anything, and he said thank you, and we hung up.

And I had never felt as happy. No drug could ever stimulate that feeling. It was unbelievable. Like I said, mind-blowing. It changed my life, opened my eyes in a big way. That was three to four years ago, and I still think about it all the time, and I wonder if he remembers too, not that it matters anyway, because I remember and that's what counts.

I share about that here because I thought it was relevant to alcoholics and sobriety. Whether it be alcoholics or just other humans in your community, or even outside your community too—anyone, really—the Big Book states very clearly that the solution is helping others who are in distress.

Anyone can fall victim as life goes on.

One thing I've heard a lot in the rooms is, we help others as a way to make up for our past misdeeds, which I understand, but that's not exactly the reason I help people. If it gets you to do the right thing, good. But I will never be able to fully make up for my past indiscretions, no matter how much service I do.

Nor do I help others because it feels good, because it doesn't always feel good. A lot of the time it feels really crappy, doing the right thing. The reason being, you don't always get to see the results of your good deeds. Most of the time, I worry endlessly if what I did helped or if it hurt. But the thing is, it doesn't matter in the end. All that matters is that I know in the bottom of my heart I did the right thing.

I do the right thing simply because it's the right thing to do. I don't seek out ways to help others, and I don't push my kindness onto others, either. When someone asks for help, I do whatever I can to suit their needs. But here's the thing: if it's not in my range of abilities or knowledge, I have to step aside or at least introduce them to someone who can better suit their needs—i.e. hand the kid over to subway security—because overstepping my bounds is a sure way to hurt someone; it will never end good, and trust me, I've overstepped my bounds on many occasions, and I will over-step my bounds again.

Because I'm not perfect.

So, in my story there are a lot of drugs, but since this is a closed meeting of Alcoholics Anonymous, I will respect those who don't have too much experience in that field and keep my story mainly focused on my drinking, which has been with me my whole life. I do have to say I would prefer drugs over alcohol, but in the end drinking was always my go-to drug because it was the easiest to get a hold of.

I've done a lot of terrible stuff that I will never be able to pay back. I was a terror in Boston, I was a terror in Rutland, and I was a terror in all the places I've travelled to throughout the course of my life, because I lived off of chaos and destruction and to me love was dead and I would make sure it stayed that way. I remember drinking in a park with some friends and I went berserk, which was a common occurrence for me, and they tried to calm me down, saying they loved this park and they didn't want to attract the attention of the police, and so, in response, I kicked over a table and screamed, **Destroy what you love!** I kicked it over, and I kicked over a chair too, and I kicked over another chair, screaming once again, **Destroy what you love!** Because I had to destroy love before it destroyed me.

237

And it did destroy me; I was a sucker for girls and love and I liked to cuddle and screw and do all that fun stuff, but love always broke me down and kicked my ass in the end.

So as a result, I was a madman. I stabbed a friend in the arm because he reached over and tried to snatch one of my beers after I told him no. He told me later that if I ever got my hands on a gun, he would run far, far away. I carved a slit down a girl's neck—she was the sister of one of my band's drummers—because she barged into the room while we were practicing and told us to turn it down, and I hurled my knife at her, which **whoosh**ed past her head, thumped against the wall, bounced and twirled once, and landed on the floor. When I went to retrieve it from its spot on the floor, bending over to pick it up, that girl standing behind me, pissed off as all hell, she sent her foot straight up into my nuts, and I didn't even think, I had no time to think; I just whirled around and grasped her neck in my hand and banged her into the wall. I slammed her into it and she grunted. I said to her, very simply, **If you ever do that again** ... but I was cut off by my girlfriend's voice saying that this wasn't a very fair fight because I had a knife and she didn't. I wasn't planning on doing anything to her, though; I was just going to bang her up to teach her a lesson. But my girlfriend sauntered over to her and put her own knife in the girl's hand, and before she could even think about attacking me, I released her from my grip, lifted my knife high up in the air, and then brought it down across her neck.

Then there was the guy I stabbed in the woods in Beverly, MA, when I went out drinking with my girlfriend's friends. There was this big dude who showed me all his scars from his days as a backyard wrestler, and he was the oldest and a total prick and I witnessed him punch a younger guy in the face and the younger guy did nothing to stand up for himself. So when I jammed the knife into his thick neck, I became a sort of hero in that town and many years after, my girlfriend would tell me that random people—people she had never met before in her whole life—would come up to her at the mall and ask if she was the girl who dated the crazy guy from that night, who stabbed the big dude out in the woods. And the reason I did it, which I'm sure the rumors had forgotten about, was because he kept going into the woods to fetch more firewood,

and he kept calling my girlfriend to come and help him,

and when we left those woods together and stepped into her car,

she told me he was an asshole and he forced himself on her.

I remembered she had a steak knife in her car because she'd gotten something lodged between the seats and needed it to get the item out, and I retrieved it and headed back into the woods.

When I got out there and stood before this big dude who was only a couple inches taller than me but many feet wider and a lot more muscular, I said something which I can't remember, and he got mad and threw his arm back, but I ducked away from his punch, slid the knife out of my sleeve, and threw myself at him, knocking him over like I was some kind of rabid pit bull, and even after I lodged the blade in his thick neck, I continued to pummel him.

I got on top of him, punching him like crazy, as if he were one of those training balls that boxers used and would punch and punch and punch as it bounced and bounced and bounced and looked like a blur because the boxers would pound it so fast; and as my fists pelted him like hail, lightning-fast knuckles dropping on his face, I held the handle of the knife in my hand.
The only reason he didn't die there was because I lodged the blade deep in his neck,

> which stopped the bleeding some.

You see, I've done a lot of bad things. I've always been a menace. One Halloween night, this guy asked me, **Is this all you ever do, go around and terrorize whatever town you're in?** I said, **Yep,**

> then heaved a pumpkin over

my head and hurled it through a window.

> The window shattered,
> the lights turned on,
> and my best friend at the time and I

>>>>>>>>>>>booked it.

It was like a march of destruction.

One night we were drinking in a field and we saw the red-and-blue lights spiraling in the distance. *You all know what that means.* We all split up—there were probably about five or six of us at the time—and hid in the nearby bushes as the cop car rolled into the park, slowly easing its way into the field, splashes of light, changing from red to blue and back, creating circles on the otherwise dark grass.

My Story: The Short Version

It rolled in to the park, and all of us watched, crouched low and out of sight, as the cruiser sat there and continued to shine its flashing lights which opened holes in the darkness.

It was a frightening experience, but a regular occurrence in my life: running from cops, hiding out until the coast was clear, vaulting fences and sprinting through people's backyards.

Soon enough, the cruiser spun around and ambled out the way it came in, and we all emerged from our hiding places, sighing and relieved.

We went and finished our drinks and hit the streets for one of those marches of destruction. I swear we tipped a few cars on this march, we punched holes in picket fences, and we smashed windows. And slashed tires too.

Slashing tires was one of my most favorite things to do back then.

A girlfriend of mine was in a bad mood one night, so I took her out to a parking lot down the street from my parents' house, handed her this thick-bladed knife, and said, **Here, knock yourself out.**

We were drunk, of course.

She looked at me and from her expression I could tell she was puzzled. So I took back the knife and drove it deep into a tire, then pulled it out as the tire hissed and produced a thick, powerful stream of air that brushed past my face, and rammed it through a window. Since the blade was rather thick, I managed to shatter it in only one stab. I gave her the knife again and she took my lead. There were maybe twenty vehicles in that lot and we hit each and every one of them, leaving as the only evidence splashes of blood here and there. Fortunately, that call never came where a cop found my blood at a crime scene and needed me to report to the station for questioning.

I've done some really terrible things and, thank God, I'd only been caught for the petty stuff.
       Like the reason I came to Vermont, for example:
I was drinking with some high school kids and my best friend who was twenty in a park down the street from my parents' house—this park was located right next to the parking lot mentioned above—and as the night drew to an cnd and those kids had to get going, my best friend and I started back to my parents' house, where he had parked his pickup truck, and suddenly heard that numbing sound I'm sure you're all familiar with—

that **wee-woo, wee-woo** sound which always makes my skin crawl when I hear it, so sudden and stark that still to this day it makes me shudder and freeze up

—and of course, around the corner rolled the owner of that sound, a black-and-blue squad car with flashing lights and all.

My Story: The Short Version

I only remember short fragments of what happened there and even in those fragments everything seems fuzzy, like a watercolor painting.
One of the four cops who'd arrived on the scene—there were two cruisers in all—asked us how old we were.
                                        I told him twenty-two
                        and my best friend told him twenty-one,
and when he checked our IDs, he called us both liars and off we went, chained up in the back of a cruiser, waiting to be tossed behind bars for the night.
They charged me with Delivering Liquor to Persons Under 21/
                        and him with Destruction of Property—I
guess the reason they were called in the first place was because he had punched a hole in the window of a car in that parking lot.
Luckily they didn't know about the high school kids, whose booze was paid for by them and purchased by me, and who I only drank with because all my friends my own age had gone off to college or gotten married or had jobs that kept them from going out and getting wasted, which is something I tried so hard to avoid.
                        Responsibilities only keep people tied
                        up and one thing I never wanted to be
                        was tied up, unless I was tied to two
                        bedposts and some girl brandishing a
                        thick leather whip stood over me.

Those are just a few examples of some of the really nasty stuff I've done. I wanted to give you enough examples of the kind of person I was before I really delve into my story, so you can get a better grasp of what I became from all this.

We all have our stories of degenerate behavior, mixed in with lots of drinking and drugs, which some people say is the route of all our problems, but I say that's complete crap. I mean, alcohol is only a symptom of my alcoholism. I didn't drink alcohol and then suddenly become an alcoholic. It wasn't like I took that first drink and loved it so much that I decided I would, from then on, destroy my life. It wasn't like that at all. My life was already on its way to a big heaping pile of nothing—the kind of nothing that included jails, institutions, and death. My fate always involved flashing lights, steel bars and steel toilets, straightjackets and padded cells, and caged windows.

Before I got into drinking, I stole a lot.
I was a big thief.
During my last year of middle school, some of my friends and I decided that throughout the course of the year we would steal random items from our teachers and on the last day we would sit down somewhere and set it all ablaze.

We sat behind the high school tennis courts on the last day at that school, having skipped the whole day to do so, and we flicked our lighters like crazy, but we couldn't get the items to light—not flammable enough, I guess—so we ditched the idea and headed to the mall and I swear I stole over two-hundred dollars worth of items that day and didn't get caught. Ironically, I realized I owed a teacher five dollars and I had that money with me and I was all ready to pay her back that day before we decided to sneak away, because I wasn't a liar, or at least I wasn't then, and I didn't borrow money if I wasn't going to pay you back—but I would steal from you and laugh as I set the stolen items on fire, even though the plan didn't actually work—so my two closest friends at the time and I all headed away from the mall and toward the school, and when we got back there, we were obviously caught red-handed for skipping classes that day, and we were sentenced to spend the remainder of the day in the meanest teacher's classroom, until she kicked us out for flinging pencils across the room at her.

And I still remember all the commotion going on outside the room, kids laughing and having fun, enjoying their final day attending this school. Groups of happy go-lucky preteens would stroll right past the classroom we were in, and they would all be smiling and laughing, and I envied them, I really did.

I wished I could be out there having fun with them. But I couldn't, because truth be told, I wasn't one of them.

I was a scoundrel, a filthy cretin in their eyes—the eyes of the popular kids.

That's how it went for me.

But I was good at making friends, though. Other kinds of friends. Not kids like them.

Misfits.

Which brings me to the first time I got drunk. I mean, I drank since I first could walk. As the saying goes, anyway. I used to steal shots off the tables at family parties because something about those shots seemed intriguing; after all, it's what the adults all did, and it seemed mostly accepted, and I just wanted to be one of them, accepted and popular. But I didn't know what it meant to be drunk.

I went to the Dominican Republic with my family, and at the Dominican Republic, we stayed in a resort where I met a lot of misfits from various states, and I really liked some of those kids too—

                        I met the first girl
I ever loved, and
she and I walked
all day one day, or
at least I remember it being a
whole day.
>>>>>>>>>>>>>>>>>>>>>>>>>>>>One night before dinner—
and this was probably my third night there—I drank two rum-and-cokes, and at dinner I stole two full bottles of wine that I planned to drink when all my new friends and especially that girl I was madly in love with and I got together on the beach later on.

                  So the day turns into the night
and the stars shine bright in
the sky and the waves of the
ocean lap at the sand as it rolls
into the shore and twists
around and heads back out into
the ocean and beyond. It was a

really beautiful night. I sit in a
half-assed circle of misfits, and
I'm drinking that first bottle of
wine, feeling all right at this
point, but I've felt better and
I'm starting to wonder what
the big deal about drinking is.
I'm about halfway down the second bottle of wine and I **blink**
and the wine is gone.

Just gone.

Vanished.

And now I'm absolutely
hysterical because this is the
first time I've ever been drunk
and everything seems almost
dreamlike, unreal, and my
wine has somehow vanished,
and I stand and scream about
someone drinking my wine,
and I'm pissed, really freaking
pissed, and when I give up
screaming because I know at
this point nobody is going to
step in and admit to drinking
it—when I give up and sit down,
calmer now, the world looking
almost kaleidoscopic through
my drunken eyes, everything
seeming ghostly in the way
that it is smoky and transpar-
ent and real, and the people
around me looking all dis-

torted, their shapes moving in
hallowing arrays as if this is a
movie and I'm watching it on
TV, a really visceral movie that
I can feel and smell and touch
and it feels so unbelievably
good—when I go to sit down
and nearly miss the bench I
was aiming for, someone tells
me, **You drank it.**
And that's when I learned about blacking out.

And I had so much fun that night, more fun than
I've ever had in all my life.

And I nearly raped the girl I loved because
she didn't love me back, I think, and with my hand in her
shirt, and her saying to me, calmly, **I'm about to scream
rape,** I drew back my hand, and I don't think I've ever
been more worried about what I might do, because in the
years to come, all my morals and values were drowned
out by a thing called booze, and I loved every minute of
it. I spent the remainder week and a half at the Dominican Republic drunk, and I just wanted to keep doing it, I
wanted to devote my life to this magical thing, because
the thing is, when I was drunk, I could do all the things I
wanted to do, but that my anxiety-stricken mind kept
me from doing otherwise.

(As I grew older and older and
less and less inhibited, and
alcohol became less of a social
lubricant and more of a necessity, I got to the point where
alcohol was unnecessary if I
wanted to do crazy stuff be-

cause my mind got really
warped over time and I just
stopped caring.))))

And there were a lot of drugs too, which is why I'm going
to skip ahead to when I was twenty-two and facing five
to ten years in prison
and my lawyer said to me—and I still remember these
words exactly because it was a life-changing moment,
when I stood outside that courthouse, smoking that cigarette, and I'll tell you, I wasn't even scared at the time,
because in my mind, in my drug-addled conscious, I believed consequences were inevitable and I would end up
in prison one way or another; it was all a matter of
time—my lawyer said to me that morning, **I'm a good lawyer, but I'm not a miracle worker. Get yourself some help.**
I just stood there, with not a care in
the world and nothing to lose—you know, a lot of people
say they had lost everything in their drinking, but you
see, for me, I had nothing to lose to begin with and when
you have nothing to lose, the world is your orchard and
you can do just about anything, and I mean

anything

———so I stood there, and when he said that to me, very
stern and serious, and I could tell he was serious because his expression was slanted and firm and would
have frightened anyone else, but not me, I had no fears—
when he said that to me, I only smirked and a slight hint
of a chuckle sneaked through my lips, just slid out of me
uncontrollably, like a humorous breath. And I shrugged

and chucked my cigarette into the street and went home and got drunk.

I eventually came to Spring Lake Ranch, over in Cuttingsville, VT, and for the first two years, convinced that my problems had nothing to do with drugs and alcohol because, after all, they were my friends and they always made me feel better than how I was already feeling, I cheated prison and I screwed around constantly, not taking a thing seriously; I lied a lot, I made promises I couldn't keep, I did a lot of shitty stuff, and then some, just to protect my using habits.

The reason I came to AA in the first place, aside from my introduction to the program when I was nineteen and trying to kick a daily crack habit, was to convince others I was serious about this and basically to get them off my back, so I could continue to use and not go to prison, which was my fate anyway, I thought, so did it really matter what I did?

I guess it was my open mind that saved me, or at least that's what my therapist claims. You see, I've always had a very open mind, and even though I went to AA for all the wrong reasons at first, the seed was planted and I listened with an extremely open mind. Only I was nowhere near willing and even farther away from honest.

Two years before all this, I
slashed the tires of the car that
belonged to the only girl I *truly*

ever loved, because earlier in
the night, after breaking into a
sex shop and stealing a bond-
age belt and selling it to a
friend for five dollars, and after breaking into a car and
stealing the stereo but after
nobody bought it and just
stared at me like I was some
kind of freak of nature, tossing
it into a nearby dumpster, and
finally, after verbally assault-
ing a cop for reasons I can't
seem to comprehend this day,
calling him a series of horrible
names, some of the meanest
names in the book, until a
friend pulled me away into the
dispersing crowd and asked
what the hell was wrong with
me—after all this, two kids
jumped me and I remember
blood was dripping out of my
ear when a friend of mine
found me lying there and
helped me onto the train, and I
rode it back to Newton, back to
my parents' house, where her
car was parked, and I staggered
over to it, knife in hand, thinking it was all her fault that
those two kids had jumped me,
her fault for leaving me alone

to zigzag down the street, past
the alley where those two kids
hid, waiting for me to come by,
and when I did, the first of the
two kids darted at me so fast
he looked like a flash zipping
down the street toward me, and
I didn't see his fist go up but I
felt it smashing into my head,
and I was taken completely off
guard, plus I was drunk, so the
force of it knocked me straight
down and my head hit the
ground and bounced, and his
friend joined him and the two
of them stomped and punched
and stomped and punched me
until they saw that cop coming
and then took off running, and
the cop who came over was the
same cop I had verbally as-
saulted earlier on, and I still
remember lying there, looking
up at that cop, at his blurry
face, wanting to ask for his
help, to *plead* for his help—

*please, Officer, I just got beaten up really badly and I can't move
and I'm bleeding and it hurts so badly and I know I offended you
by all those nasty words I used but I hope you can forgive me
and help me up off the street*

    —but I was too drunk and
scared and couldn't say anything, and he just walked away

and left me there—so when I
reached her car, parked on the
side of the street at my parents' house, I thrust the knife
through all four tires and then
sat on the curb and cried.
I was bleeding and bruised and I had never felt so alone
and I knew she would be so freaking pissed at me but I
didn't care at all.

The next day she called me and I told her that I needed
help and asked if she would help me—and I told her all
this, my sad sob story to make her feel bad for me—all
of it *before* I told her about her tires, hoping that she
would feel so sorry for me that she would forget about
the fact that she had to pay a shit-ton of money for
brand-new ones, but instead serve to comfort me.

But that didn't happen; she was outraged.

Her mom drove her to pick up her car, and I didn't hear
from her again until two years later, when I was living
in Vermont, completely strung out, and I sat in my dark
apartment, barely able to keep my eyes open and my
head afloat, and wrote her an email that said
I still loved her
and missed her
and I would do anything for her.

She eventually wrote back, saying she felt the same way,
and we reconciled and even dated again for another two
years, a really hectic two years at best. In her return
email, she said she was sober, only she wasn't counting

pot, which I assumed she was counting because she said she was *sober,* after all, and I took that as her truly being sober—and she wasn't working a program, either, so some might have considered her a dry drunk—and it was at that point I decided I would get sober for her sake.

That was when I became willing and somewhat closer to honest, but still a ways away; I still had a lot of self-discovery needing to be done before I could reach honesty——it's progress, not perfection, as they say....

I've probably taken up too much time already, so I'll cut to the point. That girl who I deeply love is out drinking again, but I'm not. I got sober for her, and she didn't stay sober for me. It sucks, and I will probably never see her again, because it is unhealthy for me to do so. This program has saved my life, and believe me, I've been through the wringer. I haven't been sober for the whole time I've been in AA, but I'm closer each time I fall on my face and push myself forward again.

Some people don't make it back to the rooms, and others take years to come back. Me, it only takes a nightly adventure of, basically, me doing a face plant, and then realizing that I have to go back to AA, because I don't like falling on my face much and for the most part AA keeps me from doing so.

So I got a sponsor today. When I first started working with this sponsor, my ass was on fire and I worked hard, but today I'm kind of on the edge of complacency. I write, I read, and I've even written two books, self-published and all, since having come to these rooms, and I owe that all to AA, my sponsor, and other select individuals who have been there for me on my journey, and who have held out their hand for me and hoisted me back up onto my feet and pointed out the best direction for me to go at the time, <u>because they, too, have been exactly where I am and know pretty much what to do from here.</u>

Too Quick

Sometimes I'm in a bad mood and I'll make really harsh comments
       I'll admit/
comments racially charged   sexually charged   hateful and mean, but that's only cuz I'm a human being and I'll be the first to admit that I have problems. But when some leftist Nazi hears my angry comments and comes on my Facebook page saying how offense that is and/or how sick that is and   I'm wrong for saying that—so wrong
it only makes me feel worse. I mean, I already feel like shit and then some self-righteous NIMBY (**N**ot **I**n **M**y **B**ack**Y**ard) chimes in calling me an asshole—
       What problems does that ever solve?

You wanna come at me all high and mighty telling me I'm wrong. Why not do the noble thing and ask "What's the matter?" "Is there something bothering you?" "Here, cry on my shoulder for a minute and tell me all about it." But no....

                                   Instead I always hear, "You're wrong, you're the bad guy, you're fucked in the head, you're sick"

       sick
       sick
       sick
Why don't you point your accusing finger somewhere
else for a change?   like maybe inward because
that's where the real problems lie—inside yourself>>>>
Is the blame game really the answer to anything?
       Huh?!

                    **   ⏳   **

Last night I wrote something racially charged on Facebook saying that I hate interracial breeding—which is
true, to an extent—but today I realize I only said it because I was tired, I had a throbbing headache, and I had
just gotten off the bus where for the last half an hour a
black baby, being coddled and soothed by a white woman,
probably his mother, cried and cried and cried, so loud
and obnoxious and my head hurt and I just wanted to
strangle the infant.
See, that's called introspection
See, that's what I mean about pointing your finger inward....
                    I mean,
                    my older brother just married a Chi-
                    nese woman and I love the both of
                    them dearly/

                    I mean,
                    I have a friend who's black who had
                    just had a baby with a white
                    woman)))))))

Too Quick

Not that those two facts excuse me,
cuz they don't I realize. It's like being
racist and then offering a rebuttal
saying I got black friends so it's
okay....

I don't care who you are
I don't care what you think
    what you say
    what you wear
I accept all creeds   I accept all walks of life   I'm un-
couth, yes; but that doesn't mean I don't love my fellow
man and want my fellow man to prosper in life.
I'm sick I have problems and sometimes
    sometimes
        sometimes I say shit without first thinking
it over with myself, sometimes I'm too quick to speak,
too quick to judge, too quick ... period
sometimes I'm simply caught with my foot in my
mouth....

When I wrote this post, a friend gave me some really
great feedback, which he followed with: "But then, what
do I know? I just like tater tots and mayonnaise"—that,
right there, is the truth.
We know nothing about nothing; we all like to think we
know something about something, but in the end our
knowledge is moot.
    I wrote somewhere:
"We are all doing the best we can with the knowledge we
think we know!"

You can't get anymore truthful than that....

Newton, MA

I wasn't a popular kid growing up. In Elementary school
I had friends, a few of them. Can't remember their
names though. Well, except for one—my best friend:
Brian. He was a midget, and he had this cling-on problem. Every time I went and hung out with someone else,
he'd threaten to leave me, to stop being my friend, and
we'd fight about this. I don't know what his hang-up was,
why he was so protective of me. Could have something
to do with him being a midget, of course. But it seems
unlikely. We were just kids.

> I went to summer camp. The first camp I
> went to was Camp Grossman, a Jewish day
> camp, where I didn't make a whole lot of
> friends. I made a few, but not too many.
> The next camp I went to was an overnight
> camp, a big step up from a camp where I
> took the bus to and from on a daily basis.
> This camp too was a Jewish camp, called
> Camp Avoda. My brother paved my way
> there, he had a lot of friends who he still
> talks to today. One of the best men for his
> wedding he met at Camp Avoda. Me, I had
> two friends—*only* two friends. I went there

for one summer and one summer only, and
I made two friends—the fat kid and the
nerd with glasses. I guess that ain't too bad.
Two friends are a lot for some. I learned
from these two camps that Judaism is just
not right for me.

Later on I went to a neutral camp
called Tohkomeupog (Toke-come-you-pog).
I'll get to that later.

So, then came Middle School, at which I learned the
definition of being popular. The lesson came hard and
unexpected. I don't know what happened to Brian by the
time I got to Middle School; I haven't put too much
thought into it. The first school dance came around, and
that's when I learned all about popularity. The girls se-
lected which guys they liked, which guys would from
then on be popular.

That left me and Adam and Eric.

Oh, and Luke, but he was a little too despicable for
even me back then.

if I get the facts about all this wrong and you are dis-
pleased with that, then I've got an idea for you, don't
read this crap

Okay, so me and Adam and Eric. The three amigos. We
stuck together like a Band Aide on a wound. We had our
own fun. Eric and I, for example, we made claymation
movies with Eric's camcorder. Adam and I watched
wrestling on the TV and had our own matches in the living room. Stuff like that.

As I got older, and the cruelty of popularity in Middle School persisted, we started to go our separate ways. I started hanging out with a tougher, rougher crowd, who for the most part didn't like me much in the first place. The only reason I stuck around was because of Jay; he was like the baddest boy in our school, the older kid who'd stayed back a few years and had been kicked out of a few different schools. His first day at our school, we hit it off. He really liked me for some reason, and I knew I wanted to be his friend. I think I might have been his first real friend at that school, when I think about it. But then he met more kids like him, and right away they hit it off, and next thing they were all hanging out, all the troubled kids together like it was supposed to be—with me along for the ride. Remember, most these kids bullied me when I was younger.

I smoked weed for the first time at Jay's house, with these kids.

Weed was fun; I liked it. Then I eventually started drinking.

Drinking was fun; I liked it.

One day at Gym class, I remember sitting on the bleachers and the aforementioned despicable Luke was sitting behind me. I turned around and noticed he had a small bottle in his hand and was taking sips. I asked him, What's that?

Vodka, he said.

No way, I thought.

I moseyed up the two or three steps dividing us and said, Can I have some?

He shrugged and handed me the bottle. I took a sip—it really was *vodka*—as he reached in his backpack and grabbed another.

Where'd you get these?

My mom, he said, sipping on the other bottle. I stole them from her.

This began another friendship that brought me on my journey to fuckupdom.

i've had many different best friends throughout the course of my life, probably because, now that i look back on it, i didn't view people as individuals, but as a means to an end

as a way to gain

if you had something i wanted, i'd team up with you to get it

yeah, i know, i was a sleazy fuck back then

Anyway, that's aside the point.

My point is, I wonder if the friends of my earlier years were only my friends because of one thing and one thing only—we were unpopular.

We didn't have a whole lot in common, but we still ended up with each other. We were stuck with one another whether we liked it or not.

At the other camp I went to, the one I stuck with, I had another best friend by the name of Aaron. He and I got picked on a lot even

there. I had more friends at this camp
though, not just Aaron, but the two of us
hung together like fingers crossed. One big
thing we had in common was that we each
went through puberty later than our peers,
so for a long time we each spoke in a higher
voice.

Years after I stopped going to
Tohkomeupog, I reconnected with Aaron, after he and I had finally gone through puberty; after our balls and voices had both
dropped. I remember we saw a movie, but
that was about it. He lived somewhere in
New Hampshire, and I lived in Boston; he
drove down to Boston, and the two of us
drove out to Natick to see a movie. That was
the last I'd seen of him; we just didn't have
much in common anymore since we presently spoke in a lower pitch.

Adam, one of my two best friends from Middle School,
contacted me recently on Facebook; we reconnected,
talked for a bit, and agreed to meet next time I went to
Boston, which I had forgotten about the last few times I
was down there. Maybe the next time, though.

Between me and Eric, I have to say Adam has a lot
more in common with me, even now. He always prided
himself on not drinking or doing drugs when we were
younger. I don't know, times change, people change, and
lives just simply change. I met some guys once who said
they went to college with Adam. Real strange guys. I
met them at around two in the morning at the Newton
Center train station, when some friends and I had de-

cided to stay out all night and were currently spraying the tracks with Starter Fluid. After that night, I did a lot of drugs with those guys.

Anyway, they told me Adam drinks a lot now.

I thought it strange to hear, but like I said, people change.

Adam and I have a lot more in common because of our musical interests. He was always into Rock and Roll and Metal, played guitar, and had an AOL Instant Messenger screen name that was Rocksnotdead; that was the kind of kid he was.

Me, I listened to Rap and Hip Hop back then, but today I listen to Punk Rock, which in a way is very similar to Metal.

Eric, however, what did we have in common anyway? I guess when you're younger it's easier to find commonalities between you and your peers, considering life is so simple when you're a kid—and especially if you have no other choice.

Last time I saw Eric, I was drunk at the Newton Highlands train station. I was with a couple friends, and we were sitting on the steps that led to the street. Then the train stopped in front of us, the doors slid open, and off walked a familiar face, all dressed up neat and prim like a good little boy should be. He was with two or three friends of his own, and I said hi as they ascended the steps, and he acted like he didn't even know me. I suppose in a way he didn't—we were entirely different people then.

He always did well in school, he went off to a good college, and according to Adam, he's engaged—or he was engaged. Last time they spoke was when they were nineteen, and Adam says he's engaged. I don't know if that means now or then.

I tried contacting him via Facebook recently, and he didn't respond.

I tried again tonight, and I'll see what happens.

Why does it matter if he responds? you might be asking.

It doesn't matter if he responds. I'm just curious what became of him. If he doesn't respond, I'll probably just shrug and brush it off. It doesn't matter in the long run/

Like I said, we don't have a whole lot in common anyway.

I guess one of the consequences of living in Newton (a small town big enough to be called a city)

Newton, MA
where you are either awesome
or just an asshole

is that if you're a nobody, you will remain a nobody until you get the FUCK out of there, and find your own kind.

Period.

The end.

Punk Rock

I was always a troubled kid, spent sixth grade and on in
SPED classes, with all my fellow miscreants, all my fellow fuckups, nutcases, and retards—I was always des-
tined to the land of nowhere, to the nothingness that you
find in dark, dirty alleyways, in the back of dive bars, on
roofs and beneath bridges, and on deserted beaches en-
crusted with filth and grime....

I was a thief a loser and a freak, a kid with a mean attitude but with a heart as soft as mold.

That was my life.... That was what I lived for—trouble:
creating it and finding it, looking in all the wrong places
at first, but even so, it always felt so completely right to
me. It always felt like home.
You see, I never felt accepted in my "real" home: I had an
older brother who I always felt compared to and like I
could never live up—for he thrived at sports which I
failed at, couldn't keep up with on my slow and clumsy
feet, with my lack of hand-eye coordination, my brain
and body wasn't designed for the fast-paced, competitive
world of team sports; and he always received excep-
tional grades at school and obtained a slew of good
friends, and what with my non-verbal learning disabil-

Jeremy Void

ity and absence of reading comprehension skills, at
school I failed miserably which earned me a count of
zero friends, because no one wanted to hang out with the
failure I had become and I guess always was, as this was
in elementary school (or grade school for those who
lived in the prior generations)—and I had a younger sister who fell neatly behind my older brother, in that she
thrived in school, obtained an equal amount of friends,
if not more, and even flourished with sports.
Then there were my parents, a dad and a mom who I
recognize now did the best they could with me, but having a toddler who tended to lean away from being
hugged by his own freaking parents must have been
rough on them; I mean I reeled away from their at-
tempts at hugging and coddling me. Guess I just didn't
like being touched, I was told by my current therapist, as
there's a rare case of kids who would act that way when
being touched by their parents because they didn't want
to bc hugged.

So I was always much of a fuckup before the trouble began.

I always liked the taste of alcohol and the burn as it
slithered down my throat well before I understood what
it meant to be drunk. I remember rather clearly when
my mom caught me for stealing shots off the table at a
family party—shots set up one per place setting—and I
remember rather clearing her clutching each of my
arms in one of her hands and scolding me and I didn't
understand
I just didn't understand
I didn't want her to touch me

Punk Rock

she didn't understand me
more like it....

So the streak of trouble fit neatly into my life. I was the square peg that people tried to fit in the round hole— and the more they forced it in, thwacking and pounding and racking it as hard as humanly possible, the more it dinged and dented and became ill-fit for that hole—and trouble was in fact the square hole that people tried to steer me away from because the round hole, according to them, seemed much more fitting for me, as my brother and sister slipped into it with ease so why couldn't I? only it wouldn't work for me, I was too deformed and demented and weird for their way of life....

So, that said, you might be thinking that Punk rock fit nicely with my troublesome ways, like it in fact encouraged my trouble
but no, it only gave me an outlet, a new path at which to direct my angst and frustration, something so foreign to the family, so strange to my peers, something so outrageous for a city like Newton, the rich and safe Suburbs of Boston I had grown up in.
So much for that....

Punk rock saved me. Almost everyday I encounter some stray fuckup, drugged-up and lost in a world filled with commercialized entertainment that only serves to make me sick, and I feel bad that they either have never encountered Punk rock or are just too damn dim to accept it in their lives.

I was just talking to a
new friend this after-
noon about the SPARC
shows that used to hap-
pen once a month at the
UU Church (I'm not re-
ally sure what SPARC
means and what it was
initially designed for;
for all I know it was just
the pseudo-name used to
house these shows un-
der), which no longer
happens because the
church raised the fee as
the result of police in-
timidation and the
townspeople's and the
church-goers' concern
that something dastardly
was happening at their
precious little church.

But the irony is, these
shows gave us lost kids
something to do, when
otherwise we'd only be
getting drunk and/or
high and starting trouble
in their town, not that
we didn't afterwards....
We were given a gift of
activity that the people
of this town seem to

have their heads too far
up their asses to see that
we need; maybe if some
of the events in this
town catered to the
young folks there'd be
less drugs and break-ins.
Maybe instead of trying
to lock up drug dealers
and throw all the users
into clinics, why not give
us an alternative—some-
thing Dianne, the woman
responsible for the
SPARC shows, and who
everyone treated with
upmost respect, offered
to this town. This is a
good things, you fucking
dolts!

So, you see, Punk rock is a good thing, it gave me an outlet at which to direct my pent-up anger, a post where I
could plug in my distaste for "normal" human culture
and let the irritation flow through so that I don't have to
go through it alone.

Plus, these kids, fellow Punk rockers, are some of the
most honest, genuine kids I've ever met. If you would
just put down your prior assumptions and give us a
chance, you might be surprised, you might learn a thing
or two, come to find out that the things that bump in the
night are in fact smart and interesting and have so
much potential——more potential than your own

wonderful kids who you tend to put on the pedestal and brag about all the good they do, about the fact that they are so good at falling in line, following rules, and kissing ass.
Where does that ever get anyone?
 A lifetime doomed to be jammed inside a tiny cubicle.

Sounds like hell to me....

So this Punk rock, this thing you hold in such low regard, made me a better person, without it I'd be even more of a clueless fuckup than I already was.
Without Punk rock I would have killed myself, and with all your closing down venues and trying to keep us off the streets, my blood would have been on you....
 Now, sit on that!

You're Stupid Because You're Stupid

A few months ago I was talking to this girl who seemed all right to me at first. We were talking about different TV shows, comparing interests, that kind of thing. She was really into reality TV shows, mostly, if I'm remembering correctly.

Everything was going swimmingly until I told her one of my favorite shows. Before I disclose what that show is, I just have to say that <u>personally I am not a fan of reality TV shows; I think they're stupid and they make you stupid. They're for stupid people, by stupid people.</u> That's just my opinion though, and as of lately I'd been learning that opinions are usually bullshit because everybody's got one and they always vary from one person to the next. As much as we like to think we're right, we're wrong for thinking that because nobody is right.

So I kept my opinion to myself. Kind of. I did speak up about my disdain for that kind of entertainment. I just didn't push it. Let bygones be bygones, as they say.

So, one of my favorite TV shows is *Family Guy*. That's how things exploded.

I told her, and she said that show is stupid. I asked why, and she said it's because they make rape jokes. So what?

I thought. So what if they make rape jokes? People can joke about anything they want, the way I see it. What one person finds funny, another person thinks is garbage. Just because you don't think the joke is funny, doesn't mean someone else can't enjoy it. Who are you to say anything is wrong, for that matter?
But she didn't give me a chance to explain my stance.
She just called me stupid.

Like I said, everything was fine until I disclosed this information. We were just having an innocent discussion about what is good TV. She had a right to her opinion, and so did I. But she didn't see it that way, apparently. I was stupid, according to her.
So, like a child, I asked why. Why am I stupid for liking that show?
Because they make rape jokes and you can't joke about rape, she said. Anyone who jokes about rape is stupid.

Let me back up for a minute. Before all this she said *Family Guy* is stupid because they make fun of everyone except white American males. I chimed in with, But isn't Peter, the main character, a fat and stupid and lazy white American male? He fits the stereotype perfectly, which means *Family Guy* is one big pun directed toward white American males.

She said, Don't even go there.
I said, Just think about it.
She said, You're pushing it.
I said, Isn't it possible?
She said, No, you're stupid for thinking that.

And then she came in with the rape-jokes argument, which eventually turned into the You're-stupid-because-you're-stupid argument.

One thing I can't stand—it's like my pet peeve—is being called stupid. Probably because all my life very few people have taken me seriously. I don't appreciate being told I am of lower intelligence than you, because chances are, you're wrong. Plain and simple. I'm very smart and tested to be in the 86 percentile in regards to IQ. Which means only 14% of America's population is tested smarter than me. And I'm getting smarter by reading all the time. So you see, I am not stupid and I don't appreciate being treated as such. Which is the number-one reason why I can't stand actual stupid people. Especially those of whom think they're smarter than they are. Know your place, is all I'm saying. Stupid people tend to use the argument: You're wrong because you're wrong. They can't argue for shit, unless you are into subjectivism, in which case their arguments do in fact hold ground. But in intelligence-ville, an argument must have objectivity. So I try to argue with them, and they always walk away feeling like the victor, thinking I'm the stupid one.

Never argue with stupid people, I say, because you'll always lose....
Like in this case, with that girl.

She kept calling me stupid, and at first I kind of just took it. I kept my mouth shut. I even tried to change the subject, because this subject was going nowhere. But every attempt at some new discussion ended with, You're stupid.

I couldn't take it.

Okay, I've matured a lot in these years. I mean, a lot. Back in the olden days I would have smacked her in the face for saying something like that, and it would have only taken one utterance of *You're stupid* for me to attack. But these days are different, and the amount I can now tolerate has expanded. She called me stupid once, and I allowed it; she called me stupid again, and I allowed it.

But being badgered like that? You're stupid you're stupid you're stupid you're stupid....
I mean, really?

So I was sitting there thinking I could really fuck with this girl's head. I only had to say one phrase and she would explode. She would be my puppet for a short time. I could get her in a lot of trouble. You see, she

278

barely let me get in a single word edge-wise before she interrupted with, You're stupid.

Should I? Or shouldn't I?

I took a sip of my coffee with trembling hands. My hands were shaking because of this decision racing though my head. I was angry too, of course. My hands shook and the coffee mug jingled as I lifted it up to my lips, and I probably spilt some on the floor.

Should I? Or shouldn't I?

I could really hurt her. And I wanted to, too. She'd be mine, under my control, and it really was that easy. She was a girl, for fuck's sake, so what could she do to me? Maybe hit me with the force of a mosquito bite, which you all know doesn't hurt and you can hardly even feel it anyway.

Should I? Or—I did it.

I wasn't planning on it though. I went to drop my coffee in the sink and leave because if I stayed there any longer I would have let her have it—
I would

On my way to the kitchen I whirled around with a pissed-off pointer finger to emphasize my point, and—

BOOM:

It's people like you who deserve to be raped.
I said it. There.

Screams came hurling out of her, one long, droning, high-pitched scream.
She surged to her feet and charged me. I was walking away, and turned around to the sound of her screaming. Her body twisted and her arm lurched behind her. Then her fist, closing in fast, crashed into my face.
Like I said, a mosquito bite. It was nothing.
But don't get me wrong, I was fucking pissed. Who does she think she is?
Someone else there grabbed her and held her back as I walked away. I heard her senseless screaming ripping through the corridor. It came out hard—much harder than her punch, I must add—and as I headed to the door I said, If you lay one more fuckin finger on me, I won't be so nice.
Then I pushed through the door and left.

** **

So the reason I brought this up is because the other day someone said they applauded me for what I'd done, because this girl, he said, was so full of herself, someone had to do something. I guess what I said made her think about things; reassess her stance.
I didn't realize I had that kind of effect on anyone.

My whole life I've been an anti-trendsetter, yet I complain that nobody buys into the anti-trends that I set. But wouldn't that defeat the purpose if they did?

So the moral of the story is, <u>You figure it out.</u>

I've never intended any morals or points in anything I write, and yet people seem to find the underlying message every single time. I don't get it.

282

The Coffee Shop Blues

It's cold.
I'm sitting outside the library waiting....
                  for what?
For them to open? Couldn't be....
Or maybe—   Naw! Not me.

I'm sitting out here because I'm bored and I got no place
else to go, nobody wants me; at the coffee shop the judgmental cunts were giving me the evil eye and I felt
unwelcome—one of the sinister cunts has a copy of *Just a
Kid* because I was feeling depressed and in a giving
mood, desperate for bonding and acceptance, and it all
goes way over my head, and upon giving it to her I even
read to her and she said she liked it, thank you for shar-
ing; but I have my doubts.
But now she was staring and cringing at me like a
freaked-out little twit thinking she's more high and
mighty than the dirty, but oh so handsome, Punk rocker
sitting on the couch sipping his coffee—
maybe she read my book and immediately tossed it
thinking it was garbage, and now she holds me in such
low regards it would be impossible to change her mind/
                or—and more likely the case

she doesn't recognize me with my new haircut and my white sunglasses covering my bright and piercing blue eyes; I mean she's only seen me, what, a couple of time, with months dividing them
                    maybe;
but I would much rather assume her sinister smile is a result of my shitty ramblings, my trashy prose and poetry—it's not *that* trashy, is it?—because if so I feel justified in my anger toward her, for she deserves it, the judgmental, blond-haired cunt, with a nice and delicious-looking ass I could see myself rubbing the skin right off of—but then again

I am awkward, and shy, and nervous, which might very well provoke an awkward/shy/nervous stance against me because how else would one react toward me? I know I would shoo me away thinking I'm a frightened fool who deserves no kindness from me; I would shun me, ignore me, not say a single word integrating the silent treatment into effect.

I don't know. Would I? <<<<Maybe I'm too hard on myself. I'm tired and wired all at once.
    exhausted + being wound up = a total headcase

        Anyway, the library is open and I think I'll go in for now and maybe come back to this later
                but I doubt it because it never happens that way, I never come back—
                        but then, who knows?

                    I sure don't....

Jeremy Void's System of Values

OPEN-MINDEDNESS

Having an open mind is one of the best things one can possess. You see, so many people—and I mean, just about everyone—claim to have an open mind, but the people who make that claim seem to have the most closed minds of them all. Take hippies, for example. A group of people founded on the values of not judging others. But the big fallacy of the hippy culture is that they look down on everyone who thinks differently, acts differently. Like most cultures, they hate the things that they don't understand. Rather than try to understand it by getting to know it, letting it into one's life to better accept it, they kick it out, push it away, and steer clear of it for the rest of their lives. Take the Vietnam War, for example. What did the hippies do to the soldiers who had come back from battle? They hurled rocks at them, shouted angry slurs at the whole battalion stepping out of the boats and onto American soil, reentering their homeland. Rather than understand that some of these soldiers, if not most of them, had no other choice—they were in some ways *forced* into the army—they chose the more hateful route; they chose to discriminate.

Jeremy Void

I always cringe every time I see a bumper sticker that says TOLERANCE, because the people who sport those stickers on their cars are the most intolerant of them all. They preach a big game, talk of acceptance and all that, but when it comes down to it, they wouldn't know tolerance if it stomped on their toes and jammed a fork in their eyes. I mean, where's the swastika in all that? TOLERANCE is spelt with a variety of cultural symbols. So where's the swastika? What, not tolerant of the Nazis, are we?

(When I speak of all this, I don't mean I am tolerant myself, because I am no different than anyone else. But I don't claim to be tolerant, I claim to be human, and by being human I am not a tolerant species. The human brain only has the capacity to view a select amount of people as individuals; the rest are categorized with blanket statements, wrapped up in labels so it's easier to cope with the population as large as it is.)

GENUINENESS

Something everyone claims to have, but very few actually live up to that title. What is genuineness? Speaking your mind even when people around you disagree or disapprove. Being yourself everywhere and at all times. I get it, it's hard to always be yourself everywhere you go. But I feel like I once reached this ideal, in that I was me *every*where. But today is different, and today I care what others think of me, and most of all, I don't want the cops showing up at my door because of something I had said or done that someone interpreted wrongly. At one point in my life, I admit I didn't care; I simply didn't give a shit because I knew my fate and I had accepted it as such: jails, institutions, and death, as they say. But today I see that that doesn't have to be my fate, and because of this realization, I find it hard to be myself at all times.

But there are select individuals that I trust enough to be myself around—very few, but that's still more than none. That's why I enjoy writing and I think all should take part in some form of art. Whichever you prefer. Because art in its purest form is genuine, which is what makes good art and bad art.

Most poetry I hear sounds like the last poem I heard and the last poem I heard sounds like the poem I heard just before that. It's mostly all the same, and it's mostly all crap. It's mostly fake, talking about flowers and rainbows because you are in denial of what is real.

On New Year's Eve, 2014, I spoke to a girl who also claimed to be a poet— something everyone I meet these days seems to have in common. Her poetry was good— considering that there are so many variables to measuring poetry that it would be impossible to say any of it is bad—but there was nothing special about it. In terms of my own poetry, she said I had a lot of talent, but why am I so sad? So angry? I'm not, I told her, then asked my friend who sat beside me, When have you ever seen me unhappy? Never, he said. So to prove my point, I sat down to write a positive poem—for her sake, which is why it came out so crappy—but it started out dark and desolate and she interrupted me before I even got to the punch line. She said, See, you can't write positive poetry. Because you're unhappy, she said. I explained, No, it's just that everything starts out negative, but as it grows, it turns positive—it shows change. Why do you think colleges look more highly upon the grades of someone who got Ds in their first year of high school and Bs in their last? It's because they showed growth, something straight-A students always lack.

But anyway, I digressed. My point is, I use writing as a way to access my most genuine self, not because I'm sad or angry all the time, but because I enjoy looking at the darker side of life, enjoy poking fun at it, laughing at it, or even dampening it so it doesn't seem to hurt as much—to hurt *me* as much. It's like if you say the same word again and again, it starts to lose its meaning. Writing about this kind of stuff—expressing myself as such—makes it easier to deal with the pain that comes with being alive.

And the thing is, I don't force anyone to read what I've written against their own will, because if anyone picks up my book by chance, they have the right to put it down. Or vice versa. I'm not at fault if they make the decision to read it. Some might argue differently, but that doesn't change what I've said. If you happen to read my book, you can be damn sure that you did of your own volition. Period.

FREEDOM

"I disapprove of what you say, but I will defend to the death your right to say it."

— Evelyn Beatrice Hall.

I was standing in a bar, and I heard someone say from behind me, Are you a Republican?

I immediately spun around, about to give it to this asshole who had dared to call me a Republican, with an index finger outstretched and on its way down, ready to punctuate each word with a downward thrust. But then I saw it was an old friend of mine—who I had come there with in the first place—and he stared at me, at my angular glare, through a hazy-eyed stupor that said, *Kiss me, I'm drunk.* When I saw it was just him, I immediately relaxed and said, No, I hate Republicans.

So, uh, then you're a Democrat? he half-asked, half-drooled.

This made me smirk. I feel the same way about Democrats as I feel about Republicans. So I told him that:
I hate Democrats.

So, you're a Republican? he shot back.

I bowed my shaking head and clutched it in my hand, thinking how foolish I felt for standing in front of this drunken fool who could only think in black-and-white terms. I opened my mouth to say I hate Republicans again,
but my girlfriend stepped in my way and said, No, he's a Libertarian.

I didn't know much about Libertarians then, and I still don't. All I know is that they believe in personal freedom, and that was just about all I could say I believed in.

See, the first two values mentioned here—open-mindedness and genuineness—both create freedom. They help freedom grow and blossom. They help it prosper. Open-mindedness allows others to be free, and genuineness allows oneself to be free.

Haha, Wasted Your Time

1.

It's 3:26 PM to the minute///   and I'm sitting in my
library, the Business is playing on my computer, and I'm
finding myself bored, and wired—bored and wired, and
do you know why.... Cuz I do in fact know the cause of
this new-found energy, what I was lacking these past
few days, and I do in fact know why I was lacking it
these past few days—

    and I'd tell you

      I really would

   but then I'd have to kill you....

Truth be told, it's a secret that nobody knows, and if you
were to find out, I might get in a lot of trouble. I'm
probably even saying too much right now, but fuck it,
this is what the book is about—a series of rants and
rambling nonsense, and if you don't like it————

   I donnnn't really care, now do I?

OK, where was I?

2.

I'm sitting in my library bored and wired and I'm writing some more nonsense.... That's my specialty....   I really do hate myself, in case you're wondering—though
you're probably not—I do I do I do I really do hate me
and my stupid fucking luck.... What the hell was the Big
Man thinking?

I wonder:

>   Why did God make me this way?
>   What could god have been thinking?
>   There must not be a GOD, you might
>   be thinking....

You wanna know what I'm thinking?

>   Of course you do
>   ///or you wouldn't be reading this crap

I do believe in God, I believe in many gods, I believe in
only one GOD<<<   I don't know what I believe||||||||||||
I don't know what to believe)))

>   I don't know
>   I don't know

I   simply   don't   know
>   ///or do I?

(((you tell me>>>>>>>

3.

I can't believe this, I can't believe you're reading this, I
can't believe you're reading this crap——I'm completely
wasting your time/

but it's completely okay cuz
              .   I'm wasting my own time in writing this....
              We're wasting time together^^^^^^^^^^
                           Will you marry me?
              Of course you won't== I'm just a grotesque
                                  ....PIG!....

Oink   oink   oink   oink

4.
Yaaaaaawwn   vomit
I'm sick, I'm bored—are you?

Of course you are=====   You're reading this, aren't you?

Phonies, Liars—ASSHOLES!

A few nights ago I was at the bar and I saw this girl Jess who used to work at the Bakery and since I frequented the Bakery myself, we became acquainted and are currently friends on Facebook and even before we became friends on Facebook she bought my first two books and said she really really enjoyed them.

So I saw her at the bar and I told her I have a total of ten books now and I'm here to read a new poem and she's here to sing an original song she told me, and anxious to show her my new book, I grabbed it from inside the cage around the window in which I had stored it while smoking a cigarette to keep it dry, and sprang it in her face, not as abrasive as that sounds though; I more nicely handed it to her and said in a giddy manner *That's my newest book I got my next-to-newest one which is a book of visual poetry and is so badass called* I Need Help: The SkullFuck Collection *in my bag inside and I'll show it to you when we go in,* and she said *Okay cool,* while perusing the book in her hand, the master copy of *The Lost Letters* (I always deem one book the master copy and write VOID on a sticker and stick it to the cover because I go to a lot of open-mikes to read my work and sometimes need to fold down the corner of the pages to mark which piece I would read there, and I don't want to crease the pages of

295

a book I was trying to sell), and she flipped through a few pages, scanned it over briefly, turned it over in her hand to look at the front and back cover, and handed it back to me and said *I want that one*, so I said *It's $12*, and she said *But I don't have the money with me now I'll contact you on Facebook and arrange to meet up with you to buy the book*, and I nodded and said *Yep*, with a series of unfortunate doubts streaming through my head.

I took back the book and snuffed out my smoke in the ashtray and opened the door to go inside, and moments after reentering the Alley, after I had already reached in my bag, rummaged through the black trash bag I had used to keep my books dry from the rain, and retrieved a copy of *I Need Help: The SkullFuck Collection*, I looked to the door and saw Jess and her friend come through and walk toward the stage, and I cut her off on her way to the sign-up sheet for the night and handed her the book and she did the same with it as she did with *The Lost Letters*—just briefly flipped through and scanned the pages and handed it back and said *It looks good*—and then continued on her way to sign her name on the lined paper clamped in the clipboard sitting atop the stool set before the stage,

and I walked away and found a seat in the back in a dark shadow to cover up my scorn, feeling totally depleted, like a fool—who would believe those claims, anyway? that she would buy my books later on when she had the money???? Right!

So I just sat there and sulked by myself for a bit.

Then I saw another guy there named Chris who currently works at the Bakery and before he noticed me he just sat at the bar drinking his money in beer, and I kinda spied on him with the corner of my eye as I

flipped through *The Lost Letters* trying to decide what to read tonight, cuz I was curious when he would finally turn his head toward me and see me there and I would tell him I was reading soon and he should stick around since he has a copy of *An Art Form: The Crass Poetry Collection* and said he enjoys it, and just as he was making a B-line for the door, getting ready to leave, he passed me there and stopped and slurred *Hey.*
Hey, I said back, only I didn't slur, my voice was as clear as daylight—kinda———and I told him I was reading tonight and he said he was just leaving and had to go home and sober up because he had to work in the morning, but I said *But I'm going on in five minutes stick around only five minutes really.*
He said *Only five minutes?* and thought about it for a moment before saying *Okay I can do five minutes I'll stick around,* as his body swayed like a narrow tree caught in an easy breeze.

Five minutes later, or maybe less, I was called up to the stage by Steve the British guy who runs the Wednesday night open-mikes at the Center Street Alley, and I stood before the near-empty bar, scanned the crowd for Jess but she was nowhere to be found, but at least this guy Chris stood dead-center in front and while I read he added a series of drunk ambient chants that came across to me, sober, as a bit foolish but funny, and still I'm thankful for the appreciation he gave me, for the acknowledgement, and I approached him when I was done and said *Thanks for sticking around,* and he said *That was awesome it was my pleasure,* and off he went, stammering out the door like the good-boy drunk he was, and then in came Jess through the door

and I thought to myself *What a cunt,* and went outside and had a cigarette as Steve picked up his acoustic guitar and strummed the same cords he plays every single week—c'mon man it's getting old—and sang the same lines of the same song and it really is getting old, play something new for a change (although to please the European kids who stumbled in loudly later on he did play "Should I Stay, or Should I Go" by the Clash [yawn-vomit-vomit-yawn]), and while standing out there smoking, this guy says to me *That was really good it was really relatable I mean I don't usually like poetry but what you read   it was so good,* and I said *Thank you,* because it meant a lot to me to hear that after the pretentious cunt named Jess humored and ignored me (although I may very well be reading her reactions poorly, so sorry Jess if you ever read this, I don't mean nothing personally)))
and he said *I love Steve to death and everything but I'd much rather hear your poetry than this,*
and again I said *Thank you,*
and he continued *I mean when you first started reading I thought to myself is this about me did he write it about me cuz it was just so relatable,*
and I said *Thank you.*
Since I saw him talking to Chris before Chris had left, I said *Are you friends with Chris?* and he said *I used to work for him why?* and I told him *Chris has a copy of my book* An Art Form: The Crass Poetry Collection *and I'm sure he would let you borrow it if you asked,*
and he said *Cool.*
When I finished my smoke and moved around the table to go inside, he poked his fist out at me for a bump and I bumped it and passed through the door and sat down in the back in that same dank shadow and listened to Steve

play those same damn songs for the umpteenth time, and I obviously got bored and picked up my bag and moved to the bar so as to absorb the light while I edited my upcoming book *Chaos Writing*. Since I couldn't find a pen in my bag or my pocket so I must have dropped it somewhere or left it at home which I am prone to do, I waved over the beautiful but oh so very poser bartender (for she dresses like a Punk/metal head what with her died hair that once was a Mohawk which she had spiked up back then and her skimpy, torn clothing and fishnet, etcetera etcetera, but talks and acts like a total ditz, smiling a phony smile and cheerfully saying *Okay*, with a giddy shake of her head and buoyant puff of her butt as I order a Red Bull and she disappears behind the bar to retrieve it for me, not to mention her preppy/jock-type boyfriend with the muscles and the hair and the perfect teeth who shows up time and time again—*please!!!*) and asked her for a pen and she cheered *Okay*, and kicked up her feet behind her as she skipped to the other side of the bar and grabbed a pen and skipped back to meet me and handed it over.

After a little while, after I had edited and checked for typos in a few different pieces in *Chaos Writing*, the annoying, belligerent Brits entered the establishment [Brits? in Rutland??? what the hell are they doing here? I could understand Killington but not Rutland, it's not exactly a hot tourist spot or anything; but then, you never know] and gathered around the dartboard and took turns throwing darts at the board and even exploded with an annoying *Hurray!* in drunk, belligerent talk every time a dart sank in the board anywhere near the target, and it was too hard to concentrate with their

nuisance of energy that filled the bar like toxic gas———
toxic gas from Europe, no less—*yuck!*———and Steve the
host only encouraged it by cheering them on and playing "Should I Stay, or Should I Go" by the Clash [yawn-
vomit-vomit-yawn] and asking them questions about
where they're from and what they want him to play
since Steve himself is British and I guess he can relate to
them on some gay subconscious level, and so I got up
with a sigh, picked up my book, my bag, and the pen I
had borrowed, and hurried off into the backroom which
was complete with a pool table in the dead center and
beyond that was a couch and a coffee table where I sat
down and made myself comfortable which isn't very
hard to do for I can be comfortable just about anywhere—only the nuisance caused by the obnoxious,
belligerent Brits in the bar played out too close to home
for me to tolerate at the moment, for it reminded me of
me—somewhat——and ...
   where was I?

Oh, so back in the pool room stood this guy named Will
and his girlfriend; Will's not exactly a friend, more like
a friend of a friend, or a friend of a few friends, for we
share multiple mutual acquaintances, and when I met
him he was with my friend Star Child and it was at some
show at the Knights of Columbus and I offered to man
the door and take people's money as they entered the
building and Star Child offered to sit with me for some
of the time and when I got there she was talking to Will
who was a good friend of hers she told me later on and
at some point he sat down with us and I read the two of
them a story called "Black-and-Blue" in *Nefarious Endeavors* which I don't think had come out yet—no, wait, it

definitely hadn't come out yet I remember now because
after I had read it to them Will had promised he would
buy the book as soon as it comes out, he wanted to give it
to a friend of his who he thought would like it
                    (he called me a "word-smith")

and two years later he still hadn't bought the book and
this kind of disappoints me but there's still time I guess
even though I doubt he will——and I'll tell you why:
                    In the back room I sat down and
continued editing *Chaos Writing*, partly listening to Will
and his girlfriend's conversation and contributing one-
liners every now and then at random intervals and they
just nodded and said *Yep*, and continued on with their
conversation like I hadn't said anything to begin with
(you see, Will's very popular, he's one of the cool kids,
he's a metal head/hardcore kid, yet he's cool and popular
and can fit in just about anywhere, only he prefers the
metal/hardcore culture over the jock/prep culture cuz
the music to him seems much more fitting and blah blah
blah he's a stupid fucking poser and deserves to be
knocked down for his sins), and then Steve—not the host,
but a different Steve—joined them and stood by them
and contributed to their conversation and they accepted
him better than me for some reasons (but Steve is cool, I
like him, he's a true metal head, he dresses in odd out-
fits, like carries bananas in his waistband like they're
guns, and dumpster-dives, and does all sorts of crazy
shit, like handing me and Nick and Hunter a bowl of pop-
corn over the fence that blocks in the patio for one of
the bars in downtown Rutland and telling us to bring it
to the bar down the street and, as we walked past the bar
he directed us to, chasing after us with a pool stick and

squeaking in his oh so very high-pitched voice that sounds almost chipmuncky but fits the part well what with his short and slender figure *Hey hey get back here with that hey hey* HEY!—he's a *true* freak, not just someone playing freak cuz it seems convenient at the time) and I can't remember how but their conversation fell onto my sampler which I had sold to Will for $2 when he finally showed interest in buying *Nefarious Endeavors* again—finally, after *two freaking years*—just for the sake of that one story "Black-and-Blue" but at the time he didn't have the money and, knowing he would never buy it in the end, I dug up my sampler from my backpack and offered it to him for only two dollars, and then he, oddly enough, hugged me for some odd reason as I headed to the door wondering why and then took off and went home for the night, and he told his girlfriend about how funny it was when the book started cuz the first scene in it consists of a guy pissing on the large window in the front of Domino's Pizza as the cashier looked on—or moreover, tried to avoid looking on—while taking an order on the phone; and I don't think his girlfriend got it because she didn't seem impressed, and I asked *Will did you read any other stories in there?* cuz there were a bunch more, like "A Bag Full of God" and "Verbal Cocaine", etcetera etcetera, and he looked at me kind of dumbly and said *Wait what there's more?* and I said *Yeah dude there's much much more*, and he nodded and I realized he must have been lying when I saw him at the Alley two weeks prior and asked if he read the sampler and he said rather enthusiastically *Yeah it's SO good*, and I said *Okay*, and walked past him and went home—although he can't be *that* good of a liar, now can he?

Phonies, Liars—ASSHOLES!

I decided it was about time I headed home anyway and retrieved my bag from beside the couch, stuffed all the contents back inside, picked it up *and* started back through the bar proper, passing Steve and Will and Will's girlfriend on my way, and I turned to Will and said *You know you should buy the entire book sometime it's really good* (I know Steve's got a copy of *Nefarious Endeavors* himself which he had bought two years ago around when it had first come out, and he had only good things to say about it when I saw him the next week at the same place), and Will said to me *I will I'll get it on Amazon I promise,* and I nodded and turned and continued on toward the door as I heard a hushed voice which sounded kind of like Will's say from behind me *But I'm not going to,* and I whipped toward him at the utterance, saw he was facing his girlfriend and then looked at me with an innocent smile, and I whirled back around to face the doorway pretending like I had heard nothing as I pushed through the bar proper and headed for the door and went home....

** **

This is a perfect example of when someone shakes your hand while pissing on your leg; pretending that they care while getting ready to stab you in the back as you walk away—a quick cheap shot to your spine that you didn't see coming;
but guess what—I did!————————

for Jess and Will both

Although
then again
I didn't sleep

the previous night
which means I was up
close to 36 hours
without sleep
and I have a tendency to
hallucinate
in those sleepless moments—

hallucinations that don't always fall in
the positive spectrum of things/

But still—
what a bunch of fucking turds....

I get the same reaction at my writer's group—everyone
always says, Oh great job, that poem was really good; but
when push comes to shove, nobody buys my freaking
books.

Sure, they all bought a copy of *Derelict America* when it
had first come out,
but now nobody ever forks me any dough for my later
books.

One woman even stated that *I Need Help: The SkullFuck
Collection* was definitely artistic, before I had finally put
it together in a book and the images just sat loosely on
printer paper in a three-ring binder; and that she

wanted me to let her know when it came out cuz she would definitely buy it.

Well,   it came out three weeks ago, and I'd seen her since then and she still hadn't bought it....

Well, there's still time I guess ...
right?

Of course, every now and then there's a newcomer to the group, who might view my books and then buy one or two but that's usually the last one they buy, probably because they read a chapter or two and then toss it on the floor and never come back to it again and over time it just gets scooted beneath the bed.
The end.

I actually left my writing group early today, although it wasn't because of their lack of support, it was because I wasn't feeling so hot; I just stood up while one guy was talking, waved goodbye to those who might have cared, and then walked out without saying a single word—just up and left ...   like that....

Although that isn't to say I haven't been thinking a lot in terms of how I just can't relate to them and when I go there I feel so isolated and alone, and I'm sure they feel the same way about me, like what the hell is this young guy doing here anyway?...

So I'm thinking about not attending the group anymore, although this one woman who *does* seem to show interest in my poetry, but not my stories she had told me, had promised last week that she'd buy three of my books next week since she wouldn't be there this week—she had said she would buy *Just a Kid, The Lost Letters,* and *I Need Help: The SkullFuck Collection,* although she had forgotten once before when she had made that same promise only I had yet to release *The Lost Letters* and *I Need Help* and only had *Just a Kid* available, although I had a few more books she could have bought too but it was only *Just a Kid* that she was interested in it seemed.

Anyway, I'll figure something out. This has gone on way too long already and I want to do something else for now. Thanks for caring. Seriously! It means a lot to me....

Letter to the Editor

Dear Rock and Roll Magazine,

I read your article about the Punk rock show last week, and I found myself slightly perturbed by it. You see, I'm a big Punk rock fan myself. No, I am more than just a fan, I am a true Punk rocker of sorts—I grew up with these kids, they grew up with me. Sure, I was mean as hell back then, but that's a given when you're dealing with any one social misfit: we all have our problems and our own ways of dealing with them———

But that's aside the point.

My point is, I know Punk rock to a Tee, I understand its philosophy, I lived its philosophy—and I still do because it never goes away——*but,* and here's the biggie—your article mainly focused on the bands that performed, with no mention of the crowd that showed up (the bands wouldn't have a platform at which to perform if it weren't for their supporters.)))))))))

I get it, I really do. You are a rock and roll magazine, and your goal is to promote the rockstars, to support the bands that played——because that's your goal.
BUT IT'S NOT THE GOAL OF PUNK ROCK
a culture created for the sake of snuffing the rock-stars....

I feel like your article did not accurately depict what an honest-to-God Punk rock get-together is all about——there's a reason we don't call them concerts; rockstars play concerts, Punk bands play shows....

Punk in the Park is Punk rock down to its basic element, and if you're going to write an article about a PUNK ROCK show, it would be best to also capture the energy that is buzzing amid the crowd, and not only the bands that played.
Yes, the bands play a part too, they're the core aspect to any Punk rock get-together, but that's aside the point. They don't mean shit without their supporters.

Let me break it down for you:
Jack Grisham, singer of legendary Punk rock band TSOL, changed his name on every album the band produced, because he felt as if his name is irrelevant to Punk rock—he felt as if the music was more important than the fame. (In our culture we remember names such as Kanye West and Taylor Smith, we don't give a shit about their music or their talent or even their mere level of intelligence; all we care about is, *Will they sell?*)

Punk rock was, and still is, attempting to break down the barriers between band and crowd. At most Punk rock shows there aren't even stages, the band plays amid the crowd, the crowd stands and dances around the band; they each play an equal part to any show....

I can't explain it any more. In order to accurately capture any Punk rock show the writer/photographer **_must_**—and I can't emphasize it any more—he/she/it/or whatever **_MUST_** feature every aspect of the event: the crowd   the band   etc.

or else the point is lost....

I mean, haven't you watched any Punk rock documentaries?
{*Decline of the Western Civilization?* or *Slog?* or *Punk & Disorderly?* to name a few}

I'm sure you've seen the Grateful Dead live an infinite amount of times.

Thank you,
Jeremy Void.

P.S. I'm a writer, and not a "rockstar," but I did in fact perform at Punk in the Park as well—I read a poem called "A King in His Own Castle," don't you remember? probably not—where were *my* pictures? where was *my* moment in your corporate zine, huh????
That's what I thought! I hope your HeadQuarters burns down at the next PUNK ROCK riot coming to your town.

P.P.S. PUNCH A ROCKSTAR IN THE FACE   now!!!

310

w/ a hard-on for trouble

1.

we were in a truck, i was only w/ em cuz of the girl, we
were in the truck & we had jus dropped her off & the
unseen was playing & i was simply sick of it, i said, NO,
WAIT, turned the volume down, & said, HEY HEY, LETS
PLAY MY CD. i looked around the truck & didnt see my
boom-box, i thought o shit, whered it go? but then it hit
me that my boom-box was in the bed.
i said, ILL BE RIGHT BACK, as the truck was pushing 70
down the highway, i said id be right back, & then
grabbed the edge of the window & hoisted myself thru
so that my butt rested on the sill & the wind hit the top
half of my body, my clothes whipping on top of my skin,
i climbed out, i scooted over to the bed, i climbed out & i
reached the bed & i dropped into it, found my box,
opened the top, & then, w/ the cd in my hand, i climbed
back inside the truck window—no harm done, no harm
at all.

2.

i went outside her apartment, she was by my side, & the
2 of us held cans of spray paint & we took em to the wall
& pressed the nozzles & right away paint sprayed all

311

over the wall as we moved our hands to paint letters &
then words & then whole phrases, we wrote profanities,
tagged offensive sayings, all down the wall, & then back
at her place i stepped thru the door & did the same in
the hallway, on the walls of the corridors, big murals
saying, FUCK YOU, FUCK OFF, YOURE A CUNT, YOURE A
STUPID FUCKIN CUNT, I DONT LIKE YOU, & that kinda stuff.
we drank outta 40-ounces & whiskey bottles, her boyfriend was a stoner who was always loaded w/ pot, we
smoked his pot & sat in her apartment, & when i checked
the time i realized i had to go. i had to go if i didnt
wanna miss the train.
outside her apartment a man was snapping pictures of
my angry graffiti art, my pst-off tags, & i had a 40 in my
hand, i said to him, COOL, RIGHT?, his head spun to face
me & thats when i realized he didnt agree that it was
cool, he said, NO, & then i said, THEN WHY THE PICTURES?
EVIDENCE, he said, THEYRE EVIDENCE. IM THE LANDLORD,
he told me, & i thought o shit, the landlord, looked at the
40-ounce i was carrying, hidden inside a brown paper
bag, obviously holding maltliquor inside, i looked at it &
thought o shit, i haveta go.
i was out the door & walking to the train—no harm done,
no harm at all.

3.
we broke into our dealers house, me & my bestfriend
did it, & my girlfriend sat in her car waiting, she was too
scared to go in too, & we searched everywhere for some
rock, crack i mean, or cocaine cuz that wud be the next
best thing, or maybe he had some pills pills pills & ill tell
you we left empty-handed, we found nothing in his

house, we called him & he didnt answer which is why we went in in the first place, we called him & the fucker wudnt pick up his phone & the door to his house was un-locked so we slipped on in, to think what if he caught us snooping around, he was a big dude too, he cud of punched a hole in both of our chests, punched a hole, lifted us up & hurled us at the wall, but nothing bad hap-pened. it was no biggie, as they say, no big deal, only we didnt get high that night.

4.
i remember pissing on the front door of this health-nut food store, the whole door was made of glass, it was 1 big window, & i pissed on it, stood there pissing on it, my friend came by, apparently he had been told to find me cuz a hiphop nightclub was jus getting out & soon tough black dudes will be roaming the street, & then my friend found me there, mid-piss, said, HEY, THERE YOU ARE!, pointed forward at a slight angle, thru the door, at the camera pointed right at me.
i saw the camera, flipped it off, finished pissing, tucked my dick back inside, & kicked a spiderweb into the door, we took off & continued to be our usual mischievous selves.

5.
then theres the girl who got raped while we slept, well thats not the actual story, jus the way she told it to the police cuz we knew the truth, & i woke up in her apart-ment the morning after, by myself in her apartment, my bestfriend & she were gone, they were chasing the

fuckin spic who ripped her off, looking for him, all over cambridge, & i sat alone in the empty apartment, feeling like a piece of crap, not knowing where anyone was, & the fact that i had shot coke in my arm for the first time the night before only made me feel worst, my stomach & my head both hurt & i wanted to die die die. o boy, did i wanna die.

my bestfriend & she came back later & they told me the story: she blew the guy in exchange for a bag of coke but he didnt fork it over, he didnt live up to the deal, he jus took the blowjob & then left & didnt come back.

i might of done the same. that girl was hot, i saw her tits, she got undressed in front of us, she got undressed & then she dressed & her tits were so nice & firm i jus wanted to suck on em, i jus wanted to touch em.

i told the police the lie, that he raped her, i told em that when they called me to take my statement, i guess my bestfriend said the same, is what he told me later on. her cx-boyfriend, a really big dude we called midget for ironys sake, who she had only jus broken up w/ a few nights before that night, & who threatened us before we left the pit, he threatened us cuz he didnt want us fuck-ing his ex-girlfriend, I wanted to fuck her, my best-friend I know wanted to fuck her—her ex-boyfriend at-tacked my bestfriend cuz we *slept* while she got *raped.* but in the end we walked away unscathed.

6.

i sat in my bestfriends house, we were not *best*friends yet, jus friends, bandmates, we sat in his livingroom w/ his other friend & his other friends girlfriend & my best friends own girlfriend was there, we drank & got

w/ a hard-on for trouble

drunk, when the girls left us i showed my 2 new friends
how to make ether, we huffed, we went for a drive.
we stopped at a friend of theirs house, he lived above a
liquor store, i envied him, i wanted his life, i wanted to
live there, above a liquor store, i wanted to be an old
man w/ 2 kids living above a liquor store minus the old
age & the kids cuz all that stuff is lame & i wud never
get old, i wud never have kids, unless i forgot to use a
condom, & i forgot to pull out & went splat inside her, i
came inside her, but if i knew that I might haveta punch
her, i might jus kick her, i wud probly do both, pummeling the pregnant bitch cuz she was fat & shes going to
ruin my life so i pummel her till the fetus dies.
across the way was a condominium under construction,
we crossed the street & my friends friend & i snuck in
thru the open doorway which had no door so it wasnt
like we had to break in or anything, we followed the
hallway thru the condominium, it led us up floors, & it
was so dark in there he & i cud barely see, we cud barely
see, my soon-to-be bestfriend stood outside & we stood 3
stories above him yelling at the fucker to come inside &
join us, we yelled, made noise, we yelled & screamed,
causing a racket, & eventually he joined us, he went thru
the open doorway which had no door.
then—*lights!*
big rays of light suddenly filled the place & we cud see,
we cud see everything, we cud see each other, we cud
barely see the source, but we knew all too well what it
was.
the police!
we knew it & we slunk thru another open doorway
which had no door, we hid there hoping the cops wudnt
find us, we hid there & we waited, still a little high, defi-

315

nitely still drunk, all of us moronically brave, i mean
who does that? who hides in a doorless closet? we do, the
cops stormed up the steps & what showed em the way
was a flashlight, the beam of which we saw traversing
the floor, climbing it like it was a rockclimber climbing
up a boulder, & then we saw the first cop, he emerged
around the corner, he held the flashlight, he emerged,
turned toward us, the light honed in on us, we stood in
that doorless closet, hiding our eyes w/ our hands cuz if
we cant see them then they cant see us but it didnt work
out that way & they slapped on the cuffs & took us for a
ride....

we were busted!

These Are My People

Last I heard, my friend Nick is in Atlanta, having taken to hopping freight trains around the country. Sold all his shit and took off—just like that. Met up with another friend of mine, Jake, in Atlanta, who had gotten arrested for having sex with his girlfriend Grace in a McDonald's bathroom somewhere on this planet, and I just saw him at the Alley in Rutland last Wednesday night, so I guess he's back in town now.

Then there's Nick's younger brother, Zack, who had just detoxed from heroin and is now living in Colorado with his mother; I let him crash with me amid his detoxing and I helped him out with that—drastically.

Tonight I just got off the bus in Burlington about three hours ago, and on the bus I met an ex-famous rapper who spends his fortune traveling the country and doing drugs, and he had on him a 3" x 3" sheet of acid—I'd never seen that much acid in my whole life—and he dosed the hitchhiker from my hometown of Newton— who had burned his down there——who was sitting across from him and detoxing from alcohol, and the acid didn't play well with his mind at the present time.

Off the bus a young, skinny guy, wearing a scarf around his neck, a striped shirt, and tight black pants, approaches the three of us and immediately joins in on our conversation so naturally it would seem almost staged—turns out, he played guitar for the Punk band Strike Anywhere.

You see, these are my people—the people the average Amerikan citizen might shun—these are the kinds of people I associate with because they are honest and genuine while the rest of Amerika is backstabbing and throat-cutting and swindling and fucking one another over———*when will it end????* Maybe when I'm dead—when we're all dead, in fact.

I could give you so much more examples of true kinship, of by-chance meetups where I felt lonely and afraid and probably even shunned by the populous, and then along comes a freak who seems to gravitate toward me for some odd reason I can't explain and we hit it off right away—once again proving that I don't fit in with the mainstream society.

So **you might think I'm crazy, you might think I'm sick—but hey I'm alive and there's nothing you can do or say to change this fact.**
We thrive while the rest of Amerika dies.

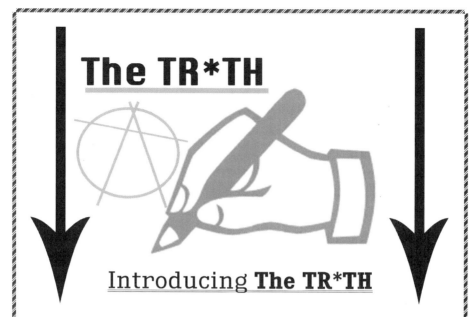

The TR*TH

Introducing **The TR*TH**

I'm sober, I'm happy——but I'm lonely, and at times I feel so utterly drab as if all hope is depleting me, and soon I'll be stuck in a nihilistic sea of angst and frustration....

But don't get me wrong, I like being sober, I like this life, I like being here, and if I wasn't me, but someone else, I'd be even worst off, I suppose.

So all this bitching and moaning from me is just what I have to do to vent at times, to let out my frustration so that it doesn't burrow deep inside me and bob its head out at the worst possible moment——

and you all know what would happen then, right?

Part 1
the world
me

Jeremy Void

i sit in unisons &
i feel the hate coming thru
the door——i sit here
bored & feeling
mischievous, menacing glares
——im BORED....
How many times must
i tell you?
im racking my fists
against the door,
my skin blistering beneath
the reverberating pelts/

i sit in the room
& its silent
& still
      & i wanna go out
      & i wanna live my life
but i have no life
to live....

my friends come & go
bustling one moment
dissipating the next....

i have a few friends
but they have no names...
theyre nameless entities
soulless demons
who will eat you
for dinner
      yum yum yum!

The TR*TH

the music plays fast
i got a headache
       I Want It Faster
or the pain in my head
will never settle....
       PLAY IT LOUDER

you dont know
you will never know
you stuff yourself w/
Facebook & YouTube
& boring distractions alike

but you dont know me ...

im alone
im alone
i sit in a dark shadow waiting
i wait forever & no one ever comes
along & saves me....
i had girlfriends but they hate me/
so whats the point? if im
not getting laid today.

I JUST GOT
BETTER THINGS TO DO!!!

a man told me what girls want.
Girls want what girls want, he sed.

i refuse to play your silly games—
I JUST GOT
BETTER THINGS TO DO!!!

321

Jeremy Void

altho it wud be nice
—WOULD BE?—
if i had me a slave
a slave who wud spread
her legs on command & let
me stick it in whenever i wanted
to.

Guess im lonely—
thats just a terminal
reality for me, but

I JUST GOT
BETTER THINGS TO DO!!!

Your life
Your hell
Your World

is not right for me.

i lived in the gutter
w/ other junkies &
scumfucs alike,
dirty & drugged out—
but today things are
different:

For one,
        IM SOBER
cuz

I JUST GOT

The TR*TH

BETTER THINGS TO DO!!!

I was a lowlife boozer
way back when
but today im a
changed man, a scholarly man
an author, but still on the lowdown
which in turn makes me a
lowlife scholar, I suppose
a literate lowlife
a lowlife higher than life
higher than you...

but I JUST GOT
BETTER THINGS TO DO!!!

Part 2
This is where the
trouble starts it starts w/
cliques, clubs, posses, or whatever//
it starts when unions are
formed, thats why i hate
PUNK ROCK
slimy cunts, all of them....

You think youre cool,
with your trendy badges
You Trendy Fucks
with your spikey, died hair
your painted black leather jackets,
you colors and your slogans
and your preaching bullshit——

last i checked, school
is not in session—so save
your preaching for someone
who gives a shit—cuz i couldn't
care less:
How much did that jacket
cost you?
        anyway

NO

I'm me, I'm no Punk
I'm me, I'm just a runt...
I'm me me me! & searching
endlessly for fun.

I JUST GOT
BETTER THINGS TO DO!!!

So I sit here going nowhere
wishing for things
just out of reach
if only they'd come a little
closer
i would be put at ease,
but its not that easy

NEVER WAS————

Part 3
THE HEADLINES read
        another man

The TR*TH

        dead
        another child
        abducted
        another young girl
        raped & beaten—
this i know—

i dont need the damn tv
to tell me this
the newspaper to spell it
out for me—

this i know....

PERIOD

The world is in crisis
STOP
the terrorists have won
STOP
DRUGS & GUNS and prostitution
rule supreme and there's
no point in fighting it...
anymore
STOP STOP STOP

this is RUTLAND
home of the junkie
You think your life
is in a rut?
Wait till youre
taking it up the butt by
robbers

and corrupt cops
and high & mighty pseudo-
hippies who think their
way is right——

I JUST GOT
BETTER THINGS TO DO!!!

in THIS world
        run by
        Facebook, run by social media
        & the like, the REAL media
        needs a way in, an avenue so
        they can continue to rape us
        with their rhetorical rubbish
so they can continue to
own our souls.

THIS IS WHAT AMERICA
is doing to you, but
today
in THIS world
        run by
        Facebook, run by social media
        & the like, the REAL media
        needs a way in, an avenue so
        they can continue to rape us
        with their rhetorical rubbish

I JUST GOT
BETTER THINGS TO DO!!!

id much rather read

The TR*TH

a book, write a poem,
learn something new, explore
a new idea—cuz a guy says to me

Saturday night, he says:
Knowledge is power....

But
today
in THIS world
     run by
     Facebook, run by social media
     & the like, the REAL media
     needs a way in, an avenue so
     they can continue to rape us
     with their rhetorical rubbish
do they really?

Knowledge might be power
but money is godliness
stupidity is royalty ...

and im smart in an age
that values dumb dumb dumb
people—what's next?
     To be rewarded for slapping your
     chest one too many times.
     To be rewarded for
     biting your own ear off....

If you pay me, I might just
leap off a roof and plunge right
into a bush—

wouldn't be the first time
I've done
such a thing.
How much money would you give me
to see me slam my head
into a brick wall?...

I was doing that for free
and now I've found that people
will actually pay good money
to see that....

Start a YouTube channel,
film me screaming at a hamburger—
bound to make millions, you know....

Part 4
I'm a hopeless romantic
on the run from
myself, tied up to one
girl
and then another
all for
        what?

its going nowhere....
I lived that way
for way too long
don't you see
Girls for girls
surfing the hot waves
of pink pleasure

The TR*TH

all for
     what?

its an endless struggle
this mindless hope
roping me in like barbed wire
I'm tangled
I'm cut
stuck in a tangle of needles
all for
     what?

im a nihilist
I believe in NOthing
but then there's something
out there beyond me
There has to be, and I pray to
it
what is it?
A Dream, a Scheme, it's got me
tied to the magazines
of love
This love

I JUST GOT
BETTER THINGS TO DO!!!

I run for cover
lurking beneath railroad bridges
with other freaks like me—
they drink their forties
I Drink my caffeine
we scream and we

Jeremy Void

shout for something
or another
      something more
      something better
We want it all

The TV promised a good life
The movies promised a
happy ending, but in this life
nothing ever ends——
it just goes on and on
swirling into madness
THIS is my madness
THIS is me
    here
        now
The only ending I know of
is in the back of a black
hearse
your body burned to ashes
and the ashes
      packed into the bottom of
a yearn
      and hurled off the bridge
      into icy waters

thats not the way I want to
go—
I do want a happy ending though
I do want some relief
but all I've got is a hand
to rub myself with as the white tears
spurt out of me

The TR*TH

like smoke>>>>>>>>>>>>>>

im sad
sick of being here....

Im alone and the
world is trying to censor me
THE TITLE OF this POEM
is TR*TH, for this is my
TRUTH, uncensored
unabashed
unrestricted
      theres too much
      friction in this world
      too much
      restrictions trying to hold us
down

and I'm plummeting
down
down
down

I JUST GOT
BETTER THINGS TO DO!!!

I'm sober now
dont you see?
I'm living the nightmare
but at least I'm
sober now......................

It

could
always
be
worst, I remind myself
when the shit hits the fan
when the riots start

and we have to run for cover

THIS IS AMERICA, my friend
and as such i want my rights///

I Want the Right to Be ME
That's the TRUTH
of it.............................

Part 5
The AMERICAN DREAM
        or moreover
        the AMERICAN NIGHTMARE
        for me....

I lived in the
AMERICAN DREAM
in Newton, Massachusetts
where you can be a star
or just a loser
        I was a LOSER
thats my AMERICAN DREAM
it wasnt pretty——
i got cornered in the locker room
after gym class where STARS

The TR*TH

surrounded me and one
put me in a choke hold
and smashed my head
into the concrete floor

The AMERICAN DREAM
      or moreover
      the AMERICAN NIGHTMARE
      for me....

I got cornered at the Store 24
and beaten with an inch of my life
as the guy threatened to kill me
      for what?
      for looking different than him?

id take my chances in Dorchester
in Mattapan
on Blue Hills Ave, with the bloods
and crypts, at war selling drugs
& guns
and prostitutes///

ive been to the inner city
a place where kids from my
hometown should not roam
ever
      its not safe
      for whom?
      Who are you trying
      to protect?

Ive always felt safer there

than I ever did in
newton<<< Home of the
AMERICAN DREAM.
The american dream was a myth
and these black kids of
the ghetto had the right idea
by exploiting it
with drugs
& guns
and prostitutes—get your sucky-sucky-
fucky-fucky
on while youre at it.

They had a vision
They had accepted it as such
They had come to realize that
the AMERICAN DREAM had no place
for them, and so
         they lived on the skids///

I JUST GOT
BETTER THINGS TO DO!!!

Everyday I see some hot chick
dressed in her skintight clothing
to show off her tits and ass
and maybe even a camel toe
         in search of
         the AMERICAN DREAM

to find a sugar daddy
to spread the wealth>>>>

The TR*TH

I haven't had a REAL dream
in years
only nightmares stream thru my mind
at night
when I sleep
because the things that I seeked
and dreamed of
all my life
i discovered later on
to be ridden with filth

I was disillusioned
my prior illusion of
        the AMERICAN DREAM
was smashed
stuffed in a blender, and I
saw a side of life most people
never see cuz theyre too busy
accepting the lie

Hey, the lie accepts them
        so why not?

But me
I saw past the lie
I had no choice
it was either that or
        get trampled by
        white men dawning blue
        suits and brandishing
        blue briefcases filled with
        paperwork//

Jeremy Void

I JUST GOT
BETTER THINGS TO DO!!!

The AMERICAN DREAM
is not what it seems
The american dream
is just not for me///

When I dream about AMERICA
the only thing I see
is red, and it fills my vision
like spilt blood
      ——that's my american dream)))

About the Author

Jeremy Void was born and raised in Boston, MA, where he played in a Punk rock band called Lethal Erection and stirred up chaos everywhere he went. Friends, enemies, and followers alike called him "St. Chaos," and he kept up his reputation at all times, finding the funny side of just about everything, and leading a life of misadventures that eventually led him down a rocky road to Rutland, VT, where he resides for the time being.

Having failed out of high school, Jeremy Void is completely self-taught in the craft of writing. He taught himself the basics—like grammar, for example, which he had very little knowledge of or prior experience with when he began his new leaf as a writer—along with more advanced tactics that prove helpful in writing short fiction or even poetry, or anything, for that matter. Although he has taken a few Creative Writing classes and a couple English Comp classes at CCV (Community College of Vermont) and a Fiction Writing class at the Gotham Writer's Workshop in New York City, and has attended various workshops/conferences in the field, most of what he knows comes from his own experimenting with words and grammar and seeing how other authors do it in the slew of novels and poems he has read in the past five years or so.

Jeremy Void

He is the author of 10 books—books written in a variety of different styles, from short fiction to short nonfiction to essays to poetry to experimental writing to visual poetry, and more. His debut book, *Derelict America,* is a book of short fiction and there are a few different essays weaved in. These stories, although fiction, are mostly based on his own experiences navigating through a drug-fueled existence. Some stories, even, could be called short nonfiction, but for all intents and purposes he has decided to call them short fiction.

Derelict America is fast-paced and thrilling from the beginning to the end; it can be crass at times but at others the words he chooses to use run smoothly and paint vivid descriptions that come to life before your very eyes. He best quality as a writer was, is, and always will be, his ability to swing words on the page smoothly and rhythmically so that in reading it one might even hear music in one's own head.

Then he came out with *Nefarious Endeavors,* which, again, is a book of short fiction, only the stories he wrote for it are even more fiction than the ones he wrote for *Derelict America.* He always says that the stories of *Derelict America* are 10 to 20% fiction and 80 to 90% nonfiction, but in *Nefarious Endeavors* the complete opposite is true; that it is 80 to 90% fiction and 10 to 20% nonfiction. There are, though, three short nonfiction pieces weaved in, which he labels as such, giving each the subtitle "A True Account." And he includes poetry in the back too, because in writing *Nefarious Endeavors* he started to get back into writing poetry after meeting a girl who was rather passionate about writing poetry herself.

In the past he had written all the lyrics for his old band Lethal Erection, and various poems on the side which had gotten lost over time, what with his lack of values and caring for anything of his own back then—with the exception of a few. So the poems featured in the back of *Nefarious Endeavors* are more like song lyrics, only without music to accompany them.

After reading a few of these poems at various open-mikes in Rutland, VT, people had approached him and said the poems reminded them of Beat Poetry.

Then, on Facebook, someone wrote, "From Lethal Erection to beat poet—the Jeremy St. Chaos story." Which rather pissed him off at first, because he was well aware that this guy was just trying to get a rise out of him, and he didn't much appreciate being the pun of a joke from a guy he barely even knew. But after rehashing what the guy said, Jeremy Void decided there might be something in there—something good and valuable—and from that point on he started reading beat poetry, immersing himself in it, and as a result his own poetry has evolved into something so amazing he can barely comprehend how it happened himself.

So he wrote *Smash a Lightbulb: Poetry for Lowlifes,* which is a slapdash collection of various things he had written after *Nefarious Endeavors,* but the majority of it is in fact poetry. Then he wrote *Erase Your Face: The Skull-Fuck Collection* and *Just a Kid* at virtually the same time. *The SkullFuck Collection* is what he calls his collection of visual poetry—which he did entirely on Microsoft Word since he had yet to obtain Photoshop on the computer. And *Just a Kid* is more poetry, plus a slew of experimental pieces, which he had started experimenting with when he was just about done writing *Smash a Lightbulb.*

But, all this time, he continued to write short fiction, getting better and better at it and the stories were getting longer and longer and starting to become unfinished, what with his short attention span; so he came out with *Sex Drugs & Violence: Incomplete Stories for the Incomplete Human*, which is a collection of stories he had started writing but never finished. Thinking it would be a shame if these stories never made it to print, for there were so many of them and some of them, even, could be considered his best work only unfinished, he compiled all the incomplete stories into *Sex Drugs & Violence*. But don't let the title fool you, for *Sex Drugs & Violence* is his cleanest, less offensive book of short fiction.

Then, shortly after that, he did *An Art Form: The Crass Poetry Collection*, which is more poetry, only much more crassly written than his other poetry. Then he did *I Need Help: The SkullFuck Collection*, which was in fact done on Photoshop since he had finally obtained it on his computer at that point; so this collection is a lot more interactive than the first. Then he did *The Lost Letters*, which is another book of poetry.

Then, finally, *Chaos Writing*....................................

Final proof 22